DRAMA & DEMOCRACY

NCQ TITLES

Legal Fictions
Politics & Letters
On Yeats: Upon a House
Drama & Democracy
Locating Theology
Time Pieces
Critical Paranoia
On Joyce: 3 easy essays
On Eliot
Literary Conversions

Film texts

A Trip to Rome
A Short Break in Budapest
Four Days in Athens
A Week in Venice
Magic in Prague
The Last Priest of Horus
WWW: the weekend that warped the world

Play texts

Darwin: an evolutionary entertainment
Strange Meetings & Shorts

Eliotics

Forthcoming

Rubbishing Hockney & other reviews
On Collecting Walter Benjamin
Autobiography & Class Consciousness
Considering Canterbury Cathedral

Though each can be read independently,
these NCQ publications, taken together,
comprise a single hyper-text collection.

DRAMA & DEMOCRACY

Bernard Sharratt

New Crisis Quarterly
2015

NEW CRISIS QUARTERLY

ncq@newcrisisquarterly.myzen.co.uk

First published 2015

ISBN : 978-1-910956-07-6

For
all my one-time
colleagues and students
in Drama at Kent

CONTENTS

Foreword

Acknowledgements

The drama of Raymond Williams:
In whose voice? A kind of letter.

The Politics of the popular?
—from melodrama to television

Towards political drama - next move?

Raisons des textes : a review

FOREWORD

This short book offers three essays concerned with the potential of various modes of drama for shaping a democratic politics. This might, of course, seem an absurdly optimistic or entirely irrelevant concern in today's media landscape.

Publishing essays is, in any case, at best a minor contribution. I once coined the phrase 'the Mrs. Gasskell syndrome' to indicate a familiar dilemma: when wondering what political contribution one might make to an issue, a writer often ends up writing about the issue in the hope of persuading readers to wonder about what contribution they might make themselves .... At least, putting together these essays has taken up little of my time and few trees will have been sacrificed for them. Whether readers will waste their own time in reading them, I don't really know. That depends partly on whether they can take my small efforts further and improve on them.

The first piece explores the drama of Raymond Williams, known for his many critical works but less so for his several plays, as well as novels. Williams wrote a great deal about drama, and it was characteristic of him that he should offer his own plays, for stage and television, as part of his overall critical-political project.

A more general piece follows, on the politics of some forms of what used to be known as popular drama. This was originally given as part of a conference I helped organise, which included not only the usual academic papers but also several performances, including a memorable working rehearsal by Joint Stock, then engaged in staging David Hare's *Fanshen*. A brief note follows, dating from involvement with a guerilla theatre group and published in *Radical Arts* edited by Bruce Birchall.

After some hesitation, I have also included a piece reprinted from my *Literary Labyrinth* which, among several other drastically over-compressed components, argues that drama had a directly political role in classical Athenian democracy. It may be thought ironical that a consideration of the possibilities of what I call 'democratic reasoning' is written in a form and style which perhaps some will find inappropriately difficult, or even inaccessible, but the issue I was trying to explore seems to me complex. I wish I had found a clearer approach.

This last essay in particular might be read in conjunction with my book *Legal Fictions*. And even possibly alongside the various film-texts and play-texts I am also publishing, with at least the intention of trying to write in a mode which deploys some popular cinematic and theatrical forms.

An essay which I wanted to include was entitled 'Drama & Politics : From Athens to the Internet'. This would have extended the argument to explore, for example, the potential of interactive games, internet video, and on-line interventions. Unfortunately, the text of this lecture, delivered at a conference, is now lost. Somebody borrowed it and only illegible scribbled notes survive.

However, the title of my imprint 'New Crisis Quarterly' revives the name of the exceedingly short-lived periodical whose first, only, and farewell issue appeared in 1984, under the guise of *The Literary Labyrinth*. Its editorial programme was to publish reviews of books I didn't feel I had the time actually to write, as with the imaginary book entitled *Raisons des Textes*. Both the variously named reviewers and the variously authored books reviewed in *Literary Labyrinth* were therefore wholly imagined, but—as some compensation—any real readers were warmly invited, if so inclined, to write the reviewed books themselves. Accordingly—in the original spirit of *NCQ* —you are cheerfully urged to compose that missing lecture for yourself, using, or ignoring, as you wish, the indications of its possible content which the other essays provide. I would also, of course, hope that you will write better plays and films than I have.

In any case, the overall invitation to readers of New Crisis Quarterly remains: to continue or complete a work if they so wish, specifically the various attempts of my ageing generation to make the relations between drama and politics a viable and effective contribution. I recall especially the work of Trevor Griffiths, David Edgar, Steve Gooch, Michelene Wandor, Caryl Churchill, but also the different but related work of colleagues at the University of Kent in setting up, in the early 1970s, a drama degree programme which shared some of those concerns, and tried to combine critical study with practical experience — among them David Bradby, Louis James, Marion O'Connor, Jill Davis, Alan Beck, Alan Pearlman, and others. Different preoccupations have succeeded ours, but the underlying problems remain and in the present critical context some of those previous emphases are worth, I think, recalling.

B.S.
MayDay
2015

Acknowledgements

The piece on Raymond Williams originally appeared, in a different form, in *Raymond Williams: Critical Perspectives*, edited by Terry Eagleton, Polity Press,1989. Reprinted with permission from Polity Press.

'The Politics of the popular? —from melodrama to television' was published in *Performance and Politics in Popular Drama*, edited by David Bradby, Louis James and Bernard Sharratt, Cambridge University Press, 1980. © Reprinted by permission of Cambridge University Press.

THE DRAMA OF RAYMOND WILLIAMS:
In whose voice? A kind of letter.

I had been re-reading *Koba*, in my much-creased copy of *Modern Tragedy*, still with some loose jottings tucked inside it from when I had, as a student, wanted to produce the play. I'd paused to think about that scene in which Ruth kills herself in front of Joseph. I was puzzled and disturbed by several different feelings and thoughts crossing in my mind. The relations between choice and pressures in any action, and the relation of gesture to meaning. Specifically, here, the problem of a gesture which doesn't, within the action, need to be 'interpreted' (it comments pretty directly on all those other deaths which Joseph acknowledges his responsibility for, while still claiming that he had 'no real choice') yet which is also, literally, a dramatic gesture, requiring response within a drama. It's even, according to some notions of theatrical convention, a 'melodramatic' gesture. And so I found myself trying to reflect upon the kind of play I felt myself to be reading — while also aware that my reading it, rather than following it in a theatrical performance, perhaps itself encouraged an inappropriately deliberated response.

But I was puzzled also by another, concurrent, strand of thought: what kind of contribution to make to this volume of essays, 'in honour of Raymond Williams'? Any ostensibly impartial 'assessment' of your work seemed quite inappropriate, unlikely, even impossible. And which work? It wasn't as an important critic or scholar of, say, drama that I wanted to write about you, but as someone who combined and connected your academic work and your socialist commitment. Yet what form, quite, could accommodate that relation?

And then — another thought crossing in the mind — I realised that it was nearly one o'clock, time for the TV news. I relaxed and switched on. The main item — it was 6th

September 1986 — was the ending of a hijack in Karachi. By a 'tragic misunderstanding', it was said, the hijackers had reacted to the lights in the grounded plane suddenly going out by presuming that the Pakistan authorities had ordered a commando assault on the plane, whereas in fact (so it was said) it was simply a generator which had failed. The hijackers began shooting. Several passengers were killed. Other news-items included: two murders in England; a bombing in France; a funeral in Northern Ireland; a report about nuclear waste disposal. I watched. And then didn't have the heart to return immediately to reading *Modern Tragedy*. I let the TV run — a *Grandstand* recording of a failed attempt on a world track record, some golf, football gossip . . . Now bored, but still without the energy or impulse to pick up *Koba* again, I flicked channels.

And, suddenly, that familiar, unmistakable voice, those apparently pained, perpetually blinking eyes, that powerfully engaged yet apparently easy style. Yourself. Contributing to an Open University programme on the differences between Lawrence's play *The Widowing of Mrs Holroyd* and his short story *The Odour of Chrysanthemums*. As I tuned in, the programme was nearly over; you were just quoting from the story:

> Her mind, cold and detached, said clearly: 'Who am I? What have I been doing? I have been fighting a husband who did not exist. He existed all the time. What wrong have I done? What was that I have been living with? There lies the reality, this man.'

You commented that this detached voice is not the only voice the story can use, that the story has several voices . . . But my attention had wandered, to the very fact of hearing your own voice, this man I had been thinking about. And, abruptly, you were concluding your contribution with, characteristically, a question left suspended: 'Who then is speaking?'

A cut, and there was Jack Shepherd (an actor I can never see without thinking of him as Bill Brand) dressed and bearded as Lawrence might have been, seated as in a set of *The Widowing of Mrs Holroyd*, reading from a book, speaking words Lawrence wrote, from the end of *The Odour of Chrysanthemums* again. Indeed, who was speaking? Shepherd read through the rest of the story and the screen faded. Credits and a date. The following Open University programme concerned the problems of industrial waste disposal. I watched, for a while. Then finally turned back to *Koba*.

*

The conjunction of these various aspects of that very ordinary moment, around lunchtime one September Saturday, seemed curiously pertinent to my attempt to offer a contribution to your quasi-*festschrift*. That pleasant accident of timing was, obviously, structured not just by the crossings in my mind, the vagaries of mood and choice, but by a whole system of communications and by an intelligible dual history, a set of converging tracks which could in principle be outlined as leading to that intersection, yet nevertheless the moment was experienced by me as a strange kind of coincidence. Several issues seemed to loom which continue to intrigue me about the mode and style of your work and its overall context.

In the question 'Who is speaking?' there lurk those other questions: What is the I that speaks? And on whose behalf might one be offering to speak? In your own writing you have characteristically offered a very personal voice and frequently an appeal to personal experience, an evoking of your own particular trajectory and history, but as, implicitly, to some degree representative. And hovering over your sustained commitment and contribution to socialist thinking has been that familiar problem of the implicit or explicit claim of intellectuals, writers, theorists, to speak on behalf of others, to arrive at a kind of coherence or fullness of response, articulated and organised to a point of consciousness which can thereby be made available to and for others, for endorsement and recognition.

Yet that overall problematic, that very mode of formulation, in terms of the self and experience, of the personal voice and presence, has been challenged and repudiated by appeal to such notions as the contradictorily interpellated, decentred subject, the dispersal of agencies into positions, of our 'selves' as the construction of several systems of positioning. That in some sense 'Raymond Williams' should be so patently dispersed, in that lunch-time moment, across a text on my knee, an image in front of me, a memory in my mind, a recorded, speaking voice, and written words from several specifiably different dates, seemed wholly consonant with that repudiation of the coherence of the centred I. And yet I ('I') was at that very point working on, precisely, a form of tribute to you, a teacher I am indebted to (who helped indeed to form my own 'I'), a man I have known, as an active and impressive individual. It would seem distinctly disturbing to be writing an affectionate tribute to — what? — an effect of a position? Yet the underlying questions can't simply be pushed to one side. For it is not just in your own 'style' of writing that there is an appeal to experience; it's also crucially and problematically there in the ways in which you have commented on other writers, and, specifically, in your work on drama.

*

Throughout *Drama from Ibsen to Eliot* [*DIE*] there's an insistence upon innovative moments in the history of drama as being the result of a certain encounter with a new kind of 'experience' which results in a painful reorganisation of sensibility, articulated in some new dramatic form, a new 'structure of feeling'. And it's this which provides the chain upon which you trace the history of drama from Ibsen onwards. *DIE* is largely organised into chapters devoted to named individual dramatists, with a prefatory chart of dates from 1850 to 1950, locating specific texts against a chronological sequence. This way of structuring the book, and the argument, rests upon an apparently obvious distinction between old and new experience, shaped as old and new structure of feeling. And, as in other parts of your work, the accompanying concepts tend to cluster around age, generation, the difference between a younger and an older generation as a primary way of thinking about the nature of a period, the nature of history as succession.

By the early 1960s, in *Modern Tragedy*, that crucial notion of 'experience' seems to have come under considerable pressure. The word itself is used in a variety of ways that it's peculiarly hard to pin down, as, for example, in these two passages:

> However men die, the experience is not only the physical dissolution and ending; it is also a change in the lives and relationships of others, for we know death as much in the experience of others as in our own expectations and endings. And just as death enters, continually, our common life, so any statement about death is in a common language and depends on common experience. The paradox of 'we die alone' or 'man dies alone' is then important and remarkable: the maximum substance that can be given to the plural 'we', or to the group-name 'man', is the singular loneliness. The common fact, in a common language, is offered as a proof of the loss of connection.

But then, as we become aware of this structure of feeling, we can look through it at the experience which it has offered to interpret. It is using the names of death and tragedy, but it has very little really to do with the tragedies of the past, or with death as a universal experience. Rather, it has correctly identified, and then blurred, the crisis around which one main kind of contemporary tragic experience moves. It blurs it because it offers as absolutes the very experiences which are now most unresolved and most moving.

> . . . It is characteristic of such structures that they cannot even recognise as possible any experience beyond their own structural limits; that such varying and possible statements as 'I die but I shall live', 'I die but we shall live', or 'I die but we do not die' become meaningless, and can even be contemptuously dismissed as evasions.

The relationship here between experience, understanding, and language is made peculiarly difficult by the focussing upon death, but it is clear that the key term is itself being stretched to cover complicatedly different areas of thought and feeling.

Moreover, the whole organisation of *Modern Tragedy* [*MT*] is very different from that of *DIE*. A compressed historical overview of what you call Tragic Ideas in Part I; then 'Modern Tragic Literature' in Part II; and in Part III *Koba*, the play I'd been trying to re-read. But in Part II — which covers much the same period and plays as in *DIE* — there is no longer a history structured primarily round individual dramatists, but rather a series of chapters devoted to different kinds of tragedy, perhaps different structures of feeling: liberal tragedy, from Ibsen to Miller; private tragedy from Strindberg to Tennessee Williams; what you call tragic deadlock and stalemate from Chekhov to Beckett, etc. There is now only one chapter devoted to just a single writer: a rejection of tragedy, in Brecht.

This new way of ordering authors and texts seems to indicate not any simple local revaluation or re-drawing of succession but a revision at a more basic level, in the very notion, now, of a range of options, a repertoire of responses, as constituting an overall 'period' (they are all 'modern' tragedy) so that at the same time one can find private tragedy being written alongside liberal tragedy, within the same (in some sense) cultural moment. You will later, of course, reformulate this in terms of overlapping and contending residual, dominant and emergent forms and feelings — though still with an implicit appeal to generational differences. But the apparently very tight relations in *DIE* between 'new' experience, new form, new structure of feeling and a 'new' period, seem to have become loosened, unhinged.

But then in *Drama from Ibsen to Brecht* [*DIB*], published in 1968, you revert in the title to a sense of overall succession and in fact retain a very great deal of the actual material of *DIE*. Many of the pages are indeed identical. But the organisation is again different, neither that of *DIE* nor that of *MT*. Part 1 of *DIB* is a 'Generation [note] of Masters', Part 2 reorders the chapters on Yeats and Synge from *DIE*, almost wholly rewrites the comments on O'Casey, adds an essay on Joyce and groups these various pieces as a section on Irish dramatists. Part 3 is then, apparently rather inertly, simply 'Alternative actions, alternative conventions', with Pirandello starting this section and Eliot — who had been the culmination of the whole argument in *DIE* — relegated simply to a chapter of this section, *an* alternative. Part 4, on social and political drama, includes some new material, particularly a chapter on Brecht. And then part 5, on 'Recent Drama', offers brief, almost review-like comments on ten disparate plays.

In that same year, 1968, you published a revised and extended edition of *Drama In Performance* [*DIP*], originally published in 1954. The focus of that book is the charting, from the Greeks to the present, of the changing relations between forms of annotation, or text, and modes of performance, or realisation, within different historical conditions and conventions. Yet given the scope and concision of *DIP*, it seems much less plausible than in *DIE* or *DIB* to see any such changes as arising from an individual confronting a new experience and finding a new dramatic form to encompass that experience. Indeed, DIP may well clarify what is intended by 'experience' in the other works.

For the danger *DIE* and *DIB* both invite is to think in terms of a simple empiricist notion, of an elementary encounter with some recalcitrant particular, some inner 'I' forging a shape for its own localisable and specific 'experience' prior to the secondary act of writing this down in a formal dramatic mode, and subsequently releasing that shaped whole for inevitably partial realisation in an essentially inadequate theatrical performance. This one-way model, from dramatist to final audience, with drama as the essential term in the drama-theatre coupling, would, obviously, be very vulnerable indeed to a charge of epistemological idealism. But in *DIP* it seems much clearer — because the individual dramatist is no longer the focus — that 'experience' might better be thought of in terms of coming to a realisation of the very nature of one's own particular culture and society. The 'experience' in question is more like living through a major historical change (and not, therefore, some specifically individual experience) and only realising the nature and scope of that change by a difficult and fundamental recasting of categories. And those categories are, in part, given in the dominant form of drama, whether in the relation between chorus and protagonists in the drama of the city-state or in the theological patternings of mediaeval mystery plays. Yet those categories are not primarily intellectual, a matter of conscious beliefs, but a shaping of emotions and feelings, of responses to particularised actions, gestures and words. Only when we do not 'know', in a sense, what our reaction to a significant gesture is, are we perhaps on the brink of that reformulation. (It may for that reason be worth adding that even after re-reading *DIP* I don't quite know what *kind* of relation you saw between the written text of *Koba* and any possible production of it.)

It might, obviously, be legitimate to seek some explanation for these changing foci of attention, and in particular for those three different ways of organising your responses to what is very much the same primary material in *Drama from Ibsen to Eliot*, *Modern Tragedy* and *Drama from Ibsen to Brecht*. It might, for example, be plausible to suggest, on your own kind of reading, that you must have encountered some profoundly new experience during these years, and that in negotiating it you had emerged with a new structure of feeling. After all, in the 1964 Foreword to *MT* you talk of wanting to 'get a whole structure of feeling and thinking into one book' and of how *Koba* is included, alongside other kinds of writing, because 'it seems now essentially to belong with them.' However, by 1979, in the Foreword to the Verso edition of *MT*, *Koba* seemed to 'belong to another area' of your work and was simply omitted.

Alternatively, perhaps one might regard each book as an intervention, a situated response. Ibsen, after all, had aroused the attention of a number of other Cambridge critics in the late 40s; your version of Ibsen and his progeny clearly contested an emerging orthodoxy. Similarly, the argument around tragedy in the early 60s, with George Steiner's *The Death of Tragedy* occupying a commanding height for a time, was enough provocation for *MT*; and the emergence of a relatively sterilised 'designer Brecht' in the 1960s demanded, perhaps, a more sharply political reading, which then helped to foster that growth of Brecht-influenced practice and theory of the 1970s.

At this point a persistent aspect of your entire output perhaps becomes most relevant: that in almost every area of work there is a continuity, a carry-over, from critique to a form of practice. *Culture and Society* quite clearly, if implicitly, writes your own work into its history; *The Long Revolution* ends with a set of proposals for advancing that long revolution. *The English Novel from Dickens to Lawrence* leaves off the inquiry just at the point, in terms of formal exploration, at which your own novels might be seen as continuing. Even *Preface to Film* was, after all, a preface to your own intended film-making efforts.

Whether in the study of literature or elsewhere, the problems and issues you choose to focus upon can always be seen as impinging upon quite definite practical tasks you feel it urgent to undertake. But it is then less a matter of getting the history 'right', in some impossibly positivist sense of scholarship, as of tracing the movement of which you see yourself as part. This placing of your inquiries within an overall project oriented to new forms of practice then shapes those inquiries precisely as a movement of the mind, an argument shaped as history. The movement continues beyond critique to exemplification, and it is this which gives a quite distinctive edge to your 'critical' writings. It also substantially explains why you can propose, in different books, quite sharply revised judgements of particular dramatists while, sometimes, offering a basically unchanged analysis of their work.

Clearly, your dramatic criticism might also be read in this way: the point of writing *DIE* or *DIB* is not finally to offer 'literary criticism', as a detached and spectatorial adjudication between existing texts, but rather an attempt so to trace a selective reading of the past as to enable other work to be undertaken, other plays to be written. *MT* makes that plain precisely by including your own modern tragedy.

But if this general claim holds, that your 'critical' work is always, at some level of analysis, directed towards substantial problems of practice you're actually confronting, it may also be true that some of the problems you locate in others' practice may illuminate your own critical problems. In *Politics & Letters* you largely agree with the summary offered by the *New Left Review* interviewers of your objections to Brecht's work: that 'the two terms of his drama remained the unmodified pair of the isolated individual and the overwhelming society ranged against the individual' or, in your own words, that Brecht 'was hardly interested at all in intermediate relationships, in that whole complex of experience, at once personal and social, between the poles of the separated individual and the totally realised society.' Yet at least in *DIE* your own argument also rests upon a certain polar relationship between the individual and a whole society, with the boundary of that whole society left undefined partly because the 'intermediate' term and concept you yourself employ — structure of feeling — seems to act simultaneously as both a mediating term and a formulation of the totality. Ibsen, for example, is never specified as articulating the new experience of, say, a fraction of the 19th century Norwegian bourgeoisie; you almost disdainfully decline any such sociological representativeness. Nor do you, as in *DIP*, deploy specifically theatrical history as indicating any intermediate grouping or sector. Instead, it seems that Ibsen simply speaks for all those who share that new structure of feeling — and that can, almost, be everyone, or no-one.

Of course, in making this point I am risking a certain parallel problem myself, since I am, after all, also trying to talk about the work of one individual — yourself. I therefore have to decide whether and in what way I might try to relate your own work to some intermediate levels of analysis within an overall society. So I can only be fairly tentative about what follows!

*

At the time of writing *DIE*, in the late forties and early fifties, you seemed to want to refuse consideration of any other kind of mediation except 'structure of feeling', but this refusal also seemed to involve you in a certain sidestepping of the issue of determination and choice. It was in 1946-7 that you were so attracted to Ibsen, precisely because of the resonance you found in his work to your own experience, as summed up in that line you quote so often: 'You come to a tight place and stick fast.' That very phrase indicates a kind of *impasse*, a sense of equilibrium between pressures and decision. The notion of 'call' in Ibsen, which you also found resonant, can then be glossed, within the work, as effectively a kind of self-imposed vocation, a task which at some level one has set oneself and yet which seems unavoidable, inescapable. In particular, you have recorded, in the *Politics*

& Letters interviews, how you have always thought of yourself, since that time, as primarily a writer, as having that call, that self-imposed vocation. The fact that you focussed your interests from that point rather upon letters than upon politics betokens an emphasis which runs throughout your writing, upon culture not as a secondary but as a primary, as having a status equal to 'the economic': in so far as both might be offered, by contrast or opposition, as abstractions from the totality, the one has as much validity, and can be as 'determining' in any specific instance, as the other. But the very notion of being 'a writer' inevitably carries certain period overtones, an implicit definition, which could again suggest a relatively direct and unmediated relation between the individual's response and the whole social experience, while the envisaged act of writing can itself seem both chosen and imposed; you speak of it taking shape as an 'impulse' and a 'disturbance'.

For someone in your position shortly after the end of the war it must indeed have seemed easier and more natural than it ever could today, in England, to regard yourself as having, in a quite palpable way, 'experienced' the whole society. To have moved from a village in Wales, itself shaped by both rural capitalism and nearby mining industry, to a Cambridge college, and from there to front-line combat, indeed from student Communist Party membership to the officers' mess in the Guards Armoured Division; to have helped liberate a concentration camp and then to have returned to Cambridge; to have edited a *Daily Mirror* style Army newspaper and then a critical periodical in metropolitan literary London; to have an Oxford university appointment yet to be teaching workers in the WEA; to have married and become a father — all this in the context of a world war and by the age most academics today would barely be finishing a PhD. This must have seemed a range of experience which needed summing up, which needed an articulated form, a conscious organisation of response, for comprehension. To have taken the full weight of that range of social experience might well have been to risk a certain crisis or even breakdown, while any impulse to become a writer would be both deeply reinforced, and yet also deeply problematic, at the level of developing an appropriate form for that encompassing experience.

It's also clear that the specific social experiences you had undergone were quite unusually shaped by distinctions between, and various definitions of, older and younger generations. After the very particular experience of student life on borrowed time (as Michael Orrom's filmed memories of your student group puts it) and then of war service, older not just in years but in what we call experience, you returned to a Cambridge again populated by much younger undergraduates. And went from that to teaching, in what we call 'Adult' Education, men and women considerably older than yourself. And, later, returned again, at the age of forty, to teach students this time much younger than yourself. You once remarked (in *Reading and Criticism*) that the problem many people face who try to write 'good' prose is that they imitate the prose norms of a generation or two previous to their own; this must have been acutely the case with your adult students. So, in those years, the temptation to conceive of history in terms of individuals or generations encountering new experiences and having to find new formulations and forms for that experience, must have been considerable, and plausible.

There is, however, another and perhaps less palatable facet of this felt contrast between young and old: that now in your sixties (receiving indeed these tributes from a younger generation) you can look back on an impressive, extensive and influential *oeuvre,* yet also look across at figures who have wielded much more direct power in this society by the time they have reached their sixties. There is perhaps a strong temptation for the teacher, the academic, to think of his or her own contemporaries as either younger or older than they are. For a Wilson or a Kinnock to become leader of the Labour Party by their mid-forties can then seem mildly astonishing. For a socialist, having made the choice, however determined, towards 'letters', for being 'a writer', and then to realise that others who made a different choice were actually exercising, in part, the power one had spent so much time combating, might lead to some acute re-questioning of the relations between 'politics' and 'letters'. You once ironically remarked, remembering a *Sunday Times* headline naming yourself and other left intellectuals as the sinister figures behind the new Labour Government, that you had never received even a single inquiry or a phone call from that Government. In several ways, your 1966 television play *Letter from the Country* seems to be concerned with all these intertwined problems.

Letter from the Country

An obvious keyword for the structure of the play is correspondence. It takes the familiar phrase, 'writing a letter to one's MP', and demonstrates an almost morality play version of what that might involve, in the figure of a Welsh teacher, Pritchard, who writes regular letters to a particular MP, Walter Dix, reminding the MP of the distance, the lack of correspondence, between what he now says and does and what he has said in the past. Pritchard thus acts as a kind of conscience, and that structural metaphor is made explicit in the play: 'no one knows what will happen if a man meets his conscience.' Pritchard and Dix do finally meet — that is the obvious 'action' of the play. But their relationship is then crossed by the related notion of the correspondent as an accredited, expert, a professional: a newspaper correspondent, a lobby correspondent, someone who acts as an official channel, part of the system of communication but also of disinformation. Dix is 'guilty' of an 'indiscreet leak' to such a reporter, concerning an overseas military base. Pritchard witnesses the 'leak', which is later publicly denied.

The various channels of communication, the networks of connection, are rendered visible in the play, from the process whereby a letter posted in Wales reaches a breakfast table in London, to the railway journeys, following a similar route, made by Pritchard to this distant and in many ways alien centre of power. We see the intersection of systems, the ways in which, for example, the educational system is crossed by newspapers and television. There is a moment in the play (which I remembered that Saturday lunchtime) when Pritchard switches on the TV in his class for a schools programme on 'Everyday Politics' and finds on the screen the MP whom he has just been to see in London. The play ends, of course, with a blockage of communication, a suppression of information, a denial of the previous, 'private' communication and then a further suppression of the newspaper report that would have made that lie public.

There are other starting points for analysis. The list of characters makes it very plain what their ages are, and the play is much concerned with the difference in response between Dix and his younger colleagues, who see the issues raised by the relationship between Pritchard and Dix in significantly different ways. There is the sisterly loyalty, to Dix, of Sally, who is prepared to see Pritchard subjected to pressure and perhaps prosecution under the Official Secrets Acts, to protect the lying denial of her brother, whose 'career' is at risk. There is an inability on the part of Paul to comprehend that Pritchard's decision to try to make public his witnessing of a leakage that has been denied is not personally directed towards Dix but is governed by a demand for democratic truth, for integrity and honesty in public life.

But also, uneasily held within the play, is a worrying problem: what the effectiveness of Pritchard's intervention might or could have been. The play seems to run up against a certain *impasse*, since it is clear that two quite different systems of communication co-exist within the political formation and that one finally has power over the other. To expose that power would require access to some other system of communication, but the 'professional' or the 'public' system is not normally or easily accessible to most of us. There is, in this structure, a general social experience, of what we call parliamentary democracy, seen not from the perspective of the Party or parliamentary 'professional' but from the far commoner viewpoint of the provincial citizen, the ordinary constituent, whose relation to 'parliament' is predominantly formal and distant, in both senses.

When Pritchard gets off the train and wanders round Whitehall and Westminster, there is a distinct sense of these centres of power as decidedly not being expressions of popular will, of popular power. The formal model of parliamentary democracy is palpably at variance with the feeling one has about these buildings. They so patently belong not to oneself but to a class, a ruling class. We can watch Members of Parliament, as Dix's TV broadcast actually recommends; we can even listen now to broadcasts direct from the House of Commons. But that is seen as a privilege, and an impotent privilege. We are, basically, spectators.

If, then, the best we can do to modify that power, is to send a letter, when in any case — through a network over which we have little control — the information upon which we might want to intervene has already been doctored, laundered, revised, adjusted, suppressed, before it ever reaches those media which are supposed to mediate, then the relation between the individual and 'parliamentary democracy' becomes ever more one of isolated powerlessness. Television is, from one angle of analysis, a precise image of our powerlessness, and the fact that we can watch that very process dramatically represented on TV becomes at a certain level a reinforcement rather than a resolution of that *impasse.*

That this play is itself actually taking place on TV indicates that it is indeed possible to appropriate some moments within the apparently dominant communication system. Ironically, though, we may well be watching the play in the immediate context of government denials or of manipulation of information in the *News* which preceded its transmission. Such a juxtaposition may then become, on a particular evening, part of the 'meaning' of the play precisely as a 'television play'.

English Prose

Some of these issues reappear in your introduction to the *Pelican Book of English Prose*, from 1969, which seems to me one of the richest essays you've published. It overlaps with a lot of your other work: it traces the same period as *Culture and Society*, from Burke to the 1950s; it obviously links up with your essay on Hume; it incorporates some of the same material as *The English Novel* (including comments, again, on that passage from Lawrence). Above all, it probes very explicitly the relation between ways of speaking and writing and possible modes of political relationship, within a historical perspective. And your analysis of that deep connection begins from a comparison between *The Letters of Junius* and Burke's *Thoughts on the Causes of the Present Discontents*. One passage has immediate relevance to *Letter from the Country*:

> What they have in common is sufficiently remarkable: the exposure of a political move made under the cover of morality. The strength of the argument in each case draws on an important assumption of public candour. Yet . . Junius relies on a distinction between public and private morality which is ultimately a matter of aristocratic convention . . the attack is then on a personal hypocrisy . . an *ad hominem* denunciation, within the moral conventions of a ruling class. [Whereas] there is a basis, in Burke, for an appeal to general principles, beyond the exposure of a personal failing within the convention. He can at least approach the moral judgement of a system of government, as something more general and important than the faults of a particular man in power.
>
> This substantial difference of political interest is

> embodied in the contrasted forms of writing. Junius, necessarily, extends political controversy by the device of the open letter: the personal denunciation put into general print. Burke, on the other hand, while no less immediate, is writing in a genuinely public way, not only referring the question to general principles, but describing a system of government as part of a public inquiry. The important shift from the style of eighteenth century politics, within a ruling class, to the style of a more public and open politics, can then be decisively observed. [Burke's] degree of generalization and abstraction is the necessary basis of a more general and abstract politics . . A genuinely public political argument could only begin when there was this kind of assertion of principles.

The relevance of this passage for *Letter from the Country* is clear. More generally, in that comment you anticipate a great deal of what Habermas and others have argued in terms of the bourgeois 'public sphere'. It would be possible to go on and situate literature, criticism, critical discourse, within some such model. But there is an element in your overall analysis which seems to me to be underplayed. This is partly a matter of implicit method.

At the beginning of the introduction, you comment on the expansion of readerships, the increase in editions of books, and copies of newspapers. But this is in effect sectioned off, as a factor not then fully integrated into the analysis. The growth in readership is associated with changes in ways of writing and those modes of writing are then directly associated with a potentiality of democracy, as a mode of public argument and discussion. Yet to bring these two factors into further relation, to close the circle, is to raise a problem about the underlying model.

In the case of both Junius and Burke there is indeed a continuity between the mode of address and the actual power of the collective or even individual addressee; Burke, after all, is in practice addressing a very limited 'public'. That continuity still obtains for later authors, but only insofar as they are writing for a specifiable audience about specifiable issues in relation to which that audience has the power to act. Thus, one could recognise in your emphasis on the ways in which naturalism as a dramatic form characteristically offers the room as the dramatic setting, and thereby tends to restrict its range of concerns and actions to those which can in some sense be represented as occurring within a room, a fairly precise consonance with the kinds of control and power which the dominant audience for that form would indeed have been able to exercise. If one tries to connect not just the readership or the size of it but the kinds of power exercised by that readership or audience, the kinds of domain over which they had some autonomous control, then the wider the readership the more restricted is likely to be the actual or acknowledged power of that readership, and in particular of any average member of it.

I could return to the history of drama, on an 'epochal' scale, with this issue in mind. On a very broad scale one might recognise that a 5th century Greek *demos* watching a play does so in an arena continuous in obvious ways with the kind of assembly space in which that same audience would have taken 'political' decisions for the 'whole' society. A mediaeval catholic dramaturgy might be cosmic in its reach but resolves itself into an issue of decision over one's own eternal future, a matter on which each individual is in a position to respond (at least until a theology of election and predestination prevails). Even in metropolitan Elizabethan drama, there could often have been a fairly direct continuity between the disposition of ranks of power within the auditorium and within the play; the opening of *Coriolanus* sufficiently indicates the possibilities here. English Restoration and French neo-classical drama are predominantly directed at the kinds of audience most likely to encounter precisely those entanglements of power and desire, in the marriage market or court intrigue, which are the subject of those socially claustrophobic dramas. Equally, bourgeois drama of all kinds tends to focus upon those issues which a bourgeois audience has within its own control; issues are often then offered at the precisely appropriate scale of, rather than 'reduced to', apparently 'personal' dimensions, of change of heart or sentimental sympathy. Ibsen's characters, for example, often come, it can be too easily forgotten, not from a politically nondescript or insignificant middle class but largely from the actually ruling class. And Shaw was undoubtedly right, commercially, to postpone the opening night of his *John Bull's Other Island* till after the Parliamentary recess!

But then the decisive extension of potential audiences denoted by the term 'mass media' perhaps breaks the continuity of that general congruence. For there is now a palpable strain when one watches, say, a television drama concerned with contemporary politics, where one's sense as an ordinary viewer of any direct capacity to intervene in the issues examined may be very weak indeed. Even more so, the repeated experience — I'm thinking here of your inaugural lecture, *Drama in a Dramatised Society* — of watching the news, those daily reports on bombings, famine, war, or high-level summits, NATO conferences, ministerial meetings, across a global horizon, while unable as spectator to immediately translate any of those problems into direct engagement, can lead to a general structure of feeling in which watching the news becomes a ritualised exercise in fatalism. It can then seem as if we are fissured between those selves who have remarkably limited individual power and those selves which can, with a historically unique privilege of access, watch not just dramatised 'representations' but real-time processes and actual events unfolding on a world-historical scale. That gap between knowledge and power becomes part of our structure of feeling. To turn from the reporting of some outrageous event (the bombing of Libya, Chernobyl, African famine, . .) and write a passionately informed letter — a letter to Brezhnev, or one's MP, or whoever — seems both perfectly possible and also utterly fatuous.

Yet the received 'democratic' modes of political access, mediation and engagement are also dominantly presented, and present themselves, as continuous with that distanced world of power represented as elsewhere, rather than (necessarily) as within the areas of immediate control open to the domesticated observer. A major problem of the relations between 'representation' (in both senses), forms of 'public' discourse, and the actual areas of effective control available to those who constitute the audiences for that discourse, remains deeply unresolved. Last week, to add apposite insult to *impasse*, a great deal of political reporting and commentary on television was devoted to sympathetic discussion of how the Liberal Party 'leadership' could, and would, neutralise or ignore a Liberal Party Assembly decision on nuclear defence policy. As I write, the Labour Party annual conference is being televised, but has just gone into 'private session' in order to finalise the expulsion of Militants. In this context, 'private' means 'no live television coverage'. A suitable case for analysis.

You once, I seem to remember, told an anecdote about the only time you met Bertrand Russell. At the end of a CND meeting there had been endless discussion as to what kind of protest telegram to send, and to whom. Russell had simply slipped out of the meeting and telephoned the American President and the Russian Premier. Lord Russell had been brought up, after all, in a household in which Foreign Secretaries dropped in for lunch, and for him Whitehall and Westminster were not alien territory but familiar family domains. That aristocratic gesture takes us back to the letters of Junius, but also to that phrase left hanging in the comments on Burke: 'public inquiry', the title of your next television play.

Public Inquiry

Public Inquiry could, obviously, be seen as an exercise in assigning blame for the train crash which is its focus. Public Inquiries are, often, seen in just those terms. I can imagine a family watching the play in that way, and debating —as in those once-popular parlour games —whose fault it was: Tom's for forgetting the starter signal, or his son David's for not relieving him at the shift-change, or the signalman's further up the line for arriving late, or young Gareth for distracting Tom with his unnecessary hooting —or even old Andrews whose points of order and amendments so delayed the Union meeting that David was late . . . This would be the familiar linking of a moral dilemma to a chain of causality, connected in individual actions and characters.

But the play clearly invites another reading also, in terms of a system as well as a sequence, interconnections as well as causes. Certain keywords both echo across categories of context and suggest a deeper connection. 'Connection' is itself one of those keywords, linking the railway sense of 'making a connection' with the sense involved in a process of inquiry. The very word 'train' is given another dimension by its linking with the kind of 'training' imposed upon, yet also interiorised by, ordinary soldiers during the war, and by the older generation of railwaymen. That interiorised training or discipline (given shape in the remembered voice of Jarvis) comes through as 'Duty', but is then in some tension with the everyday sense of 'on duty', a matter of cruelly demanding shifts (three weeks of 12 hour shift-working with no relief man available). The Union meeting is concerned with a motion to 'work to rule', to follow the regulations strictly, which itself raises the issue of how far the real 'rules', those developed by generations of railwaymen to ensure the safety of the trains, are what is actually laid down in the regulations —and whether British

Rail are themselves 'following the rules', in either sense. The Union meeting has its own regulations and rules of procedure, including the 'points of order' which so lengthen it —but 'points' are also the switch-points on the track and the term 'orders' looks two ways, to arbitrary authority and to adequate arrangements.

The crucial key term is probably 'responsible'. One sense comes through powerfully in David's memory of his Dad's pride in his job:

> This aristocracy, he used to call it to me: all the proud skilled men, the responsible men, and the trains rushing through, the signals, the uniforms.

But later David himself reaches for that other, narrower sense:

> A mistake under pressure. They're made all the time. But it's only a few jobs the mistakes can rear up, act in public, drivers, pilots, signalmen, seamen. All the others make their mistakes, but they can cross them out, chuck them under the bench, let them work themselves out till no one's responsible.

It is Jarvis, once Tom's mentor, now chairing the inquiry, who suggests a third sense, in a comment which also implicitly redefines a number of other key terms:

> The efficiency and safety of the railway system depend mainly on a system of communication, human, mechanical, and electronic, which has been built up, over generations, by experience and inquiry. It might seem to those involved that the only purpose of an inquiry is to assign blame. But if we can look at an inquiry in this other way, as not only an inquiry into error or negligence by an individual, but also an inquiry into the system of communication itself, we can come face to face with our larger responsibility.

Yet, as the camera cuts to a later moment, Jarvis continues with his 'next point' (another overtone): whether British Rail's system of recording information is detailed enough; the inquiry's recommendations will, it seems clear, include some suggestions on improving the register kept by signalmen. But this is to fall back from any adequate notion of 'our larger responsibility'.

It is the play's own system of communication, its exploitation of yet another sense of 'point', which helps to construct that larger sense of responsibility, taking us beyond Jarvis's own awareness. For the play uses the televisual possibilities of shifting points-of-view in order to bring home (in a literal sense) two different ways of seeing the entire process of which the railway is both image and part. For we see Tom both as a known, named character, with a personal and interior life to which we are given access, and also as a figure darkly glimpsed in the signal-box as we rush past in a train. We also glimpse other signalmen, other drivers, in the same way; but we also see from their perspective, ourselves as another train-load safely through the signals, as brief inhabitants of lighted compartments in the night. In one extraordinary sequence we move from Tom looking at his reflection in the dark window-panes from inside the signal box, to outside the box, looking in at Tom, and then to Tom as seen in the reflection, with Tom's voice-over:

> You get to see yourself from outside. That's the strangest part of it. You seem outside the box, looking in, and you see this man there, this man in dark clothes and you ask who he is and what exactly he's up to. What his life amounts to, up there above the line.

The moment is paralleled later, when Tom, looking down from the box at a passing train, tells David that when he, Tom, travels by train he stands up and waves if it's someone he knows in the signal box as they pass; but outside the 'division' (another resonant term) he just settles into it, takes the train for granted, forgets the men who man the lines. As he speaks, we cut to him and Tom on the train going to the inquiry; as he passes a signal box he stands up and waves but the signalman, a stranger, doesn't notice him.

This changing of viewpoint allows us a fuller recognition than usual of the double-facetedness of all working responsibilities: their taken-for-grantedness as an impersonal system of coordination and allocation of duties, yet also their immediate pressure as the lived experience of other people, as fully individual as ourselves. Yet in that very recognition is an awareness beyond the notion of 'individual' and towards a grasp of what (in two more key-terms) a 'public' 'service' might be. As the play insists, the problem is not that we 'know' this but *how* we know it. We know it, in one mode, by the value we give a life, any life. But not only when that life is over, as in the public inquiry into the fatal accident. And not only in the sharp contrasts of actual treatment when a 'working life' is over: Tom reduced to £2 10s a week pension after forty-seven years of work, while a 'failed' politician or general gets a peerage. We can sometimes grasp the deeper dependence we take for granted when 'personal' and working worlds intersect or overlap, as in the father-son relation in the play.

But the crucial effort is to know the nature of public dependence and relation on an everyday basis, as ordinary an awareness as that involved in the assumption that the train will not crash. But of course that is not only a matter of some personal change of consciousness. In another memorable sequence the signal box is transformed before our eyes into a possible alternative, in its arrangements, its technology, its resources, geared this time to (as we say) both the man and the job, but now, as David says,

> a different man, controlling a different system, in a different world. . . Not a man like us. We've sold ourselves cheap, to fit in with machines. We've felt

> guilty and broken when we make a mistake, the pressure too heavy on us. But not any more. We can take control, we can change the system. As we're bound to change it, to take the pressure off men.

Those 1960s terms, 'take control', 'change the system' again echo across, from the quite literal and specific sense of changing the system of communication and control within the signal box, to those necessary wider dimensions. If the actual ending of the play seems from this perspective like a local defeat, it is so only in the sense that a particular event seems an 'accident', merely a grotesque coincidence. Accidents, like defeats, show what has to be changed, in any fully public inquiry into their causes.

two modes

Whereas *Letter from the Country* might be claimed as leading, finally, to a sense of political *impasse*, *Public Inquiry* seems to allow a basically more hopeful political possibility. At issue, indeed, seem to be two rather different models of political analysis and action. The first might be termed a 'spectatorial' model, which can take the form of thinking of oneself as a watcher, an observer, situated in a position of more or less omniscience or ignorance concerning the global society. That can lead to a double-faceted view of one's political relation to that society: either an acute sense of impotence, of *impasse*, or a notion of action conceived of as deliberate intervention, the idea that one can and should so analyse the overall situation that one can then strategically choose where best to direct one's efforts. That model is, within the marxist tradition, basically a Leninist one, and it can involve a notion of acting as representative of, and speaking on behalf of, those sections of the society thought to be strategically central, a kind of ventriloquism for (normally) the working class. This might be termed a 'spectatorial' or 'interventionist' model of politics. Its liberal version is, precisely, Parliamentary politics.

The second model might be called the 'occupational' or 'conjunctural' model. Here the central emphasis would be on a different double-facetedness, on the intimate relation between power and responsibility which *Public Inquiry* makes clear. Insofar as one's ordinary job renders one liable to being called to account for significant consequences, that job correspondingly has a degree of power, even though the power may have become so routinised into the very job that it normally looks like powerlessness. It was an important insight of marxism that the working class as a whole necessarily has this double-faceted power, though it may (as in Strindberg's notion of realism) take a crisis to reveal that underlying relation. It is often this insight which is offered as the justification, within the other model, for singling out the working class as the strategically crucial force, although any occupational role might be revealed, perhaps unexpectedly, as newly central or indispensable, since the extent to which a specific occupation or role becomes politically important rests not upon some general rule but upon the specific combination of relations and forces operating at a particular moment. This model might be associated with notions of organic intellectuals, and perhaps even with syndicalist emphases, rather than with ideas of Party intervention.

One might, of course, think of combining both models in one's own political activity, by emphasising the importance of a choice of occupation, as strategic in its possibilities and implications. It might then be asked, perhaps, under what circumstances becoming a Professor of Drama can be regarded as an appropriate occupation for a socialist! But a more immediately useful direction to explore might lie in sketching a certain further correlation between these two models of politics I have suggested as at work in the two television plays, and the underlying arguments of, respectively, *DIE* and *MT*.

For the overall argument in *DIE* has a certain congruence with the spectatorial or interventionist model, particularly insofar as that model also describes features of the parliamentary mode of politics. The notion of history at work in *DIE* appeals to an evolutionary progression, with individuals representatively undergoing crises of articulation and integrity. The overall development has been towards verse drama as enabling a full and controlled expression of the whole range of human experience, beyond what is normally possible in speech or apparent in action. This involves, in one sense, the familiar ambition of 'a Writer' to be the spokesperson for the whole society, to articulate a fuller consciousness, from a position simultaneously deeply inside and above the social formation. This model then combines elements of consensus (speaking for a wholeness of society) and representation (not delegation), in a basically Enlightenment mode: at the core is a question of knowledge and, to some extent, of morality, of an integrity and adequacy of speech. John Stuart Mill's election manifesto might be the parliamentary equivalent of the dramatist's project within this structure of feeling.

The second model, the occupational-conjunctural, has a basically different core: that of power rather than knowledge, while also emphasising the notion of 'expertise' as the appropriate mode of knowledge, of competence in a specific sector. This goes with a different model of history, as constituted not by evolutionary stages but by conjunctural moments comprising several interacting layers of event, in what we can sometimes see simply as accident or coincidence, or as crisis. Insofar as all such layers are constantly present within the social formation and combine, in unexpected ways, to generate a moment of tension or creation, this model allows for a notion of 'choices' as between levels and sectors, a specification of one's position without seeking to occupy some totalising role. A variety of options might then constitute a particular conjuncture — until some decisive re-patterning produces a wholly new conjuncture, with its own new range, as in the impact of Brecht. The model of political engagement this looks to is perhaps that of delegate democracy, a range of sectoral expertise or interest groupings directly speaking from their own perspective.

On this reading, *DIB* would then be seen as to some extent dislodging both models but without firmly instituting another. The introduction of Brecht into the overall 'history' which *DIE* had constructed obviously refocussed the entire field, but only to the extent of allowing several categories of analysis to operate without clear inter-articulation: generational, national, sectoral, each perhaps with its own temporality and specificity. No overview seemed possible, and no totalising direction for the future. There is, implicitly, a kind of flattening of perspectives, a loss of any shared future. A politics consonant with this model, this form and structure of feeling, would perhaps have been simply an alliance or a putatively hegemonising politics, as in the attempt in the *May Day Manifesto* of 1967-8 to orchestrate and generalise a variety of expert analyses and single issue interests but without any clear strategic perspective or agreed form of agency.

But at this level of analysis, the Brechtian position might also be seen quite otherwise, as offering at least a preliminary synthesis of elements from both previous models, particularly through the notion of 'complex seeing', both as denoting the attitude of the audience and as a way of registering the divided, fissured, social nature of his characters. This emphasis is still held within a primarily spectatorial-interventionist model: the job of the spectator, in Brecht's theatre, is still to observe, from above the flow of the play as well as from within the flow, a critical observation registering potential alternatives, but still a spectator's role.

Yet, as you rightly argue, the fuller contribution of Brecht lies not just in a new attitude on the part of the audience, but in a new form of action, in which, within the construction of the plays themselves, that contradictory constitution of the characters is embodied. In *Good Person of Setsuan* we see a fairly simple working through of the ambivalence of occupational role, a double-factedness made literally visible. In *Mother Courage* or *Galileo* we see a whole action in which the victims are both active and acted upon, a complex interlock of response and responsibility. (One can then see why *Koba* follows your chapter on Brecht in *MT*).

But this reading of Brecht, with the emphasis upon spectator or action, upon complex seeing or formal construction, still tends to underemphasise Brecht's own theatrical practice, his recognition of theatre as production, as itself one kind of working or occupation, a making, alongside others. Your own emphasis upon drama as distinct from theatre leads you to some extent to underplay this, but it may be where Brecht's work is now most fully resonant for socialist thought.

Within the notion of theatre as an area of production, the particular occupation, the professional task, of the Brechtian actor can then be seen as having two crucial aspects. The Brechtian actor is not a star but a member of an *ensemble*, and, second, has to operate a certain distantiation from the role, a form of complex acting. The question which is always before us in a Brecht production is, precisely: who is speaking? A deliberately multi-voiced, dialogical dimension is given by our awareness of the distancing as well as the identification, between authorial words, actors' performance, characters' dialogue. There is a moment in *Letter from the Country* in which a 'crisis' is characterised as someone 'not being in touch with part of oneself.' The Brechtian actor, in refusing to identify with the role, maintains him or herself in a position of crisis, of critique, of criticism. Hovering here, perhaps, is a quite different implicit model of political analysis and engagement, suggesting a direction for inquiry which would certainly involve those endemically Brechtian features of much television, and the deep structure of feeling which connects television and contemporary politics.

It is crucial to Brechtian practice that in a theatre, whatever the weight of any prevailing convention against the possibility, the audience can always be addressed not only by the character but by the actor. Beyond the so-called 'soliloquy' there can always be direct address, there can even be conversation. Much 20th century drama hovers across that possibility, as has much popular theatre of the past. In that sense drama, however naturalist, however realistic, is never only representational, never simply a 'show' put on for us. It is potentially an action which involves us directly. I remember, as one vivid instance, a performance of *The Resistible Rise of Arturo Ui* in Turkey, just before the 1980 coup, in which the final anti-fascist speeches were wholly direct, from actor to audience. The theatre was surrounded by troops as the performance finished.

That such a possibility is always present in live theatre is one aspect of a much more basic dimension of drama, of work in theatre, which is brought out in Brecht's insistence upon ensemble playing. In any actual performance, there are two structures operative. There is that which is represented, acted out, made visible as an element in the diegesis, which may well be one of sharp, unrelenting conflict. And yet precisely for that to happen there must be also, and in control of the first structure, a second structure, of a deeply collaborative kind, a cooperative mode and endeavour, a working not against but with each other. For any actual performance to work, quite literally, the conventions must hold: one does not (completely) 'corpse' a colleague. Such basic conventions also govern the relations between performers and audience, and it is these always fundamental, though historically varying, conventions, involving audience-actor relations, actor-role relations, action-text relations, which you have emphasised in your work and which the term 'structure of feeling' points to.

What is then crucial is that 'socialism', for you, does seem to be most basically thought of (though no 'definition' is possible), at present at least, in terms of a possible structure of feeling, potential but also partly realised now —though I don't think you ever make the point explicitly in quite that way. You, of course, (more than most) offer outlines of socialist programmes and specific proposals, but to put the emphasis, in one's thinking about what 'socialism' is to be, upon some technological level or restructured mode of production, or even upon some particular detailed arrangement of ownership or democratic control, is, clearly, to risk the objection that since we can't, by definition, anticipate the inventions and discoveries of the future, we can't with full confidence offer even a sketch of the material life of that future society. But that is not to say that we can have no conception of what a future socialism, if any at all, will be like; for we do have some conception of what that socialism must (rather than simply 'should') be like, in order to be 'socialism', otherwise we wouldn't be involved in trying to create it in the first place.

If we then ask what is it possible for us to imagine, if we cannot imagine the specific material conditions of life, one could say that ways of relating to each other, at this basic level of shared conventions of collaborativeness which shape us more profoundly than we realise, can not only be imagined but can to some extent be realised now, against and even within the structures and conditions, the pressures of several kinds, that tend to lock us into exploitation and determine us towards competitiveness, hostility, self-interest, at the expense of others. Without at least the possibility of that other mode of relation, notions such as class solidarity or class consciousness would have little purchase on reality. Precisely the force of those pressures alerts us that for any alternative to be realised such pressures and conditions must not then obtain, in whatever specific form they may eventually be eradicated.

It might then be argued that though the particular achievements of dramatists may well be best explained in terms of the specific conditions and pressures upon them at a determinate historical moment, it is nevertheless palpably the case that plays are quite generally performed long after their initial moment of production and that we can still respond to the specific structures of feeling embodied or enacted in them. In a quite definite way, the embodied 'structure of feeling' of the play can be re-enacted for and by us, while the performance lasts. It has been a constant emphasis of your work, in several areas, that conventions of response, forms of experience, structures of feeling, are operative as and recoverable in specific modes of writing, particular forms of text.

But if it is possible for a past structure of feeling to be made available to a later period, it is also possible to claim in principle that a 'future' structure of feeling can also be made available to some degree in the present, in forms of writing and in forms of collaborative relationship. After all, that 'future' structure of feeling will be the result not of a mere passage of time, with predetermined forms waiting in the wings, but the result of human imagination and effort; we are not merely waiting for some hypostasised History to create it for us. No technical blueprint of the future may be possible (for the very same reason), but there can be a proleptic imaging of possible modes of social relationship and a certain partial realisation of the forms of feeling appropriate to those modes.

Drama, as a particularised performance of gestures, relations and feelings, reminds us of how a variety of distinct modes can be, to an extent, lived out and responded to in the present. Whereas the individual reader of past literature or the listener, or even performer, of past music may well be 'reliving' an emotional mood or a moral judgement, the actual acting-out of, say, a Restoration comedy upon stage is (according to one ideal of staging) far closer to the full re-present-ation of a past period's lived structure of feeling — whatever the current forms of theatre technology or production. On a more Brechtian notion of staging, of course, any such production would incorporate within itself precisely the awareness of historical difference: 'historicising involves judging a particular social system from another social system's point of view. The standpoints in question result from the development of society.' (*Messingkauf Dialogues*)

Where this might bear more specifically upon your own work as a socialist, is that the structure of feeling which has to be imagined, or constructed in advance, necessarily involves a relationship between the individual and the whole, even the global, society. For if socialism is to do with the supersession of various kinds of division, and most crucially of class divisions, it will necessarily involve, and be significantly constituted by, relationships between each individual and all others, of a qualitatively different kind, a mode of social relation which precisely does not have the present forms of mediation by class, national, ethnic and group interest (though others may obtain).

To anticipate that emergent structure of feeling may well be possible only apophatically, by a kind of negation. When Oedipus (or perhaps Koba) comes to realise that the relation between himself and his whole society, each other in it, is one of substantial identity, that the one and the many are at a certain level interchangeable, it may be that such a recognition is available only in a negative fashion, as 'tragedy': that the crisis of society is destructive of this individual because in some sense that single person then stands for any individual within that society. Certain features of television coverage may already make available that difficult awareness on a genuinely global scale: a recognition of the crying child in Ethiopia as both fully real, not a 'representation', and yet as fully representative of a global system and relation. Nuclear war remains, of course, the final scenario in which this awareness might be formulated.

Let me circle back at this point to my original puzzlement at Ruth's death in *Koba*. Within the play her gesture (hardly an adequate word for her suicide) is directed at Koba or Joseph, the Stalin figure; it is a way of bringing home to him, by an undeniable particularisation in terms of the single individual who matters directly to him, what is involved in those anonymous deaths of so many others. Yet insofar as the act is a dramatic gesture and therefore directed not only to the character but also towards the audience, that gesture (as, now, indeed a gesture) will have a necessarily different significance for us, the audience. We will not feel (and perhaps, by your very mode of dramatic writing, will not have been made to feel) that the death of Ruth has any specific, particularised emotional importance or claim upon us as Ruth's death —because we are not in love with Ruth. In a quite literal sense her action can only work as a form of special pleading to Koba. For an audience to see Ruth's death as significant in the way Koba is invited to, we would have to have already acknowledged that *any one*'s death has indeed that significance and we therefore would not need the message Joseph needs; in any case, of course, since Ruth is 'only' a character, we cannot 'love' her any more than we can, fully, acknowledge the 'reality' of her death in the first place. However, for us fully to be convinced of that utter equality of the one and the many, in life as in death, would be to occupy already another social structure of feeling. Perhaps, however, for the present our fullest access to that possibility remains located only in the fictional, in a certain way of writing and imagining. Which is perhaps one reason why socialism needs its professors of drama.

ending

This letter is too long already, I know. Let me leave it there, for now. The first letter I wrote to you was to ask you if I could join your seminar on tragedy. I had just handed it in to the porters lodge at Jesus College when the porter told me you were coming across the court, into the lodge. He gave you a pile of mail, reminded you that a taxi was waiting, that the Arts Council had phoned, that there was an urgent message, that you had a train to catch . . . — and that I had just handed in a note for you. You immediately put down your case, and the pile of mail, stopped, relaxed, leant against the wall, smiled, and said —as if you had all the time in the world — "Well, tell me what's in the note . . ." Across what then seemed a variety of gaps, distances and divisions, of roles, positions and powers, in that wholly alien environment of Cambridge, your welcoming response, against immediate pressures, that generous disavowal of other claims in the face of this total stranger's request and presence, seemed a gesture that needed no interpretation. I took it at the time as simply the utter generosity and patience of an exceptional teacher; I now recognise in that quietly undramatic gesture a further dimension of meaning, an anticipation of a social structure of feeling, the need for which could constantly be felt in the very rarity of the kind of relation to others which you so persistently embodied. Perhaps it was your capacity for that form of relation, now, which has made you seem, throughout, such an extraordinary representative for the possibility of socialism, already a delegate from the future.

It therefore perhaps matters less than it might have done that this letter was finished just as news of your death arrived.

*

THE POLITICS OF THE POPULAR?

— *from melodrama to television*

There are various difficulties involved in trying to relate the history of an art-form to the history of class struggle. Most attempts to do so begin from the art-object, the artefact, and seek to connect its 'content ' and/or 'form' to the conditions of its production; a work of art can then be seen as expressing, embodying, working through, or otherwise 'containing' the ideology of a social class. In Lucien Goldmann's criticism, for example, the work is grasped as the summation or intensification, the most coherent articulation, of a world-view; whereas for Pierre Macherey the work betrays, in its very silences, inconsistencies and contortions, the fissures and gaps which always fracture and undermine the dominant ideology of a period.[1]

Such approaches have difficulties with the notion of authorship; Lukacsian theories rely upon a dubious attribution of 'representativeness' to an author, while for Althusserians the 'author' tends to evaporate into a complex instance of relatively autonomous signifying practices — six textual codes in search of a typewriter.

An alternative line, which has some affinities with these Marxist approaches, has developed in recent work in 'reception theory', which has emphasised the act of reading, the point of consumption rather than of production, but here too it has proved difficult to accommodate the individual, the actual readers; it is the 'implied reader', the

---

[1] Cf. Lucien Goldmann, *Le Dieu cachée* (Paris, 1955), and Pierre Macherey, *Pour une theorie de la production litteraire* (Paris, 1966). Goldmann's work is influenced by that of Georgy Lukacs, Macherey's is indebted to that of Louis Althusser. For a useful introductory survey of Marxist literary criticism, see Terry Eagleton, *Marxism and Literary Criticism* (London, 1976).

response posited and pre-structured by the operations of the 'text', that is analysed, and critical theory thereby remains focused on the intestines of the artefact, unable to move onto the terrain of directly political concerns.[2]

The intricate methodological issues raised by these various approaches make any critical argument today peculiarly tentative, but thinking about the problems of 'popular art' may suggest a further facet, another angle of approach.

It's certainly possible to see some forms of 'popular' art as expressing the collective aspirations of a 'people', but that notion of 'the people' has to be recognised, often, as standing in for the self-definition of a dominated class struggling to identify itself against an imposed and degrading definition by a ruling class.[3] It may also be possible to offer a reading, following Macherey, of the lack of 'fit' between the different textual and dramaturgical codes at work in, for example, 'melodrama', thereby coming to terms with the sense of oscillating between the aesthetic conventions and strengths of dramatic realism and the sentimental emotionalism and moral polarisation of the strip-cartoon which emerges from reading Pixericourt, Bouchardy and their English successors. [4]

But if we try to combine the Althusserian emphasis on conditions of production with the Constance school's

---

[2] For a representative example of this approach, see Wolfgang Iser, *The Implied Reader* (London, 1976). Iser is the main figure in the 'Constance school' of 'reception theory'.

[3] Work along these lines might be developed by elaborating the notion of 'popular-democratic interpellations' advanced by Ernesto Laclau in his *Politics and Ideology in Marxist Theory* (London, 1977), esp. pp. 100-11 and 196-8. A paper given at the Kent conference, 'Punch and Judy to Andy Pandy' by Malcolm Knight, offered a similar analysis with reference to the theories of the Marxist aesthetician Sanchez Vazquez and the theatre of Dario Fo. I am grateful to Malcolm Knight for his critical comments on an earlier version of my paper.

[4] Cf. the papers by James, Howarth and McCormick in Part One of this volume.[*Performance & Politics in Popular Drama*]

emphasis on reception and seek to analyse the *conditions of reception* of 'popular' art, we may be in a position to understand more clearly some of the peculiar difficulties of creating a 'popular' political art today.

I want to try, in what follows, to suggest, in a drastically simplified way, some of the conditions of reception which seem to underpin the response of working-class audiences to a variety of forms of art and entertainment which it would be difficult not to label, in some sense, 'popular'. Part of my concern is to understand the experiences and aspirations not of the 'class' as a whole but rather of the individuals and families who comprise the 'audience' for art; it is not 'the working class' which attends a theatre performance; though an audience always constitutes a 'collective', whereby any individual response is shaped, an audience is not the same kind of collectivity as a 'class'.[5] As we enter a theatre or switch on the television we enter into relationships with others and with ourselves that cannot easily be mapped onto the relations of production and consumption that constitute the specifically economic and political identity of a class.[6] In the disharmony between the collective strengths of a class and the individual position of the members of a class, one of the functions of 'popular' art may perhaps be located. Some facets of that disharmony can be traced in this paper.

Insecurity and impotence

Insofar as the designation 'popular' indicates that the audience for a particular form of drama or entertainment includes, to some considerable extent, members of the working class, one can say that the life experience of much

[5] Sartre's analyses of different kinds of collectivities, groups and series in his *Critique de la raison dialectique* (Paris, 1960) might provide a useful starting-point for understanding the nature of an 'audience'

[6] See the points raised concerning the internal relations of production in theatre-work itself, in 'After Fanshen: a discussion', this volume.

of that audience is characterised by economic insecurity and political impotence, and that the popularity of a particular form of cultural activity may therefore be related to those components of their experience. [7] By this I mean that in the nineteenth century and in modified ways in the twentieth century one central element in the situation of a working-class family has been acute vulnerability to economic uncertainty and a lack of control over the forces governing their overall condition. In general, it has been characteristic of individual and domestic working-class life that an apparently minor event can have immediately drastic consequences: a rise in food prices may finally erase a narrow gap between income and necessary expenditure; a slight fluctuation in national or sectoral trade conditions may result in lay-off or redundancy; a brief illness, minor accident or momentary 'indiscipline' (drunkenness, 'insubordination') may result in loss of job; a wage-claim may end in a long-drawn-out and difficult strike.

This is what I might call the experiential obverse of the structural control exercised by a ruling minority over the conditions and prospects of employment. A long history of efforts by working-class organisations, by the class as collective agency, to ensure increased security and achieve some counter-balance of control can, of course, be charted; but it remains true that always at the personal level a degree of insecurity and impotence remains. In contemporary terms, this can be seen not only in the persistence of large numbers on the poverty-line or on the dole but also in a wide-spread sense of unknown or ill-understood forces affecting and governing social and economic conditions. The psychological result of this situation can be a constant,

---

[7] Obviously, 'insecurity' can be a feature of anyone's experience, but my argument presumes that vulnerability to economic vagaries is more characteristic of some social groups than of others and that it is the more insecure groups who make up the characteristic audience for 'popular' art. Cf., however, Douglas Reid's analysis of audiences in his paper in this volume.

if latent, sense of fear and of living in a state of permanent risk.[8]

Escapism, dream and nightmare

One familiar way in which a link has been suggested, or presumed, between working-class experience and popular art-forms is the notion of 'escapism': that in enjoying certain forms of entertainment, sport or other activities, an economically deprived audience seeks 'escape' from mundane pressures and anxieties into a world of fantasy, day-dream, wish-fulfilment, or simply an obliteratingly colourful and spectacular excitement; a variant of this interpretation emphasises the 'release' of pent up emotions in an exaggerated or vivid form.[9]

---

[8] For aspects of the argument in this paragraph, see, for example. *Power in Britain*, ed.J. Urry and J. Wakeford (London, 1973); *Elites and Power in British Society*, ed. P. Stanworth and A. Giddens (London, 1974); M. Benyon, *Working for Ford* (London, 1973), especially ch. 7; K. Coates and R. Silbum, *Poverty: the Forgotten Englishman* (London, 1970); F. Wilson, *Dockers* (London, 1972); T. Lane and K. Roberts, *Strike at Pilkington's* (London, 1971). One aspect of working-class insecurity in nineteenth-century London has been explored in the analysis of 'casual labour' in G. Stedman Jones, *Outcast London* (London, 1971). For an exceptional example of local control by nineteenth-century working-class radicals, see the analysis of the Oldham situation inJ. Foster, *Class Struggle and the Industrial Revolution* (London, 1974). One might also bear in mind some lines from two plays: 'A man stands up to his neck in water, so that even a ripple is enough to drown him' (David Hare, *Fanshen*), and 'At one point it looked as if they were going to go back to work and suffer defeat at the hands of the American imperialists, so their Sandra could have a white wedding' (John McGrath, *Fish in the Sea*).

[9] Cf. e.g. R. Dyer, *Light Entertainment*, BFI Television Monograph 2 (London, 1973), especially quotations on pp. 10—11, and ch. 3, "The Aesthetics of Escape'. It is possible, incidentally, that certain forms of emotional reaction only seem 'exaggerated' to those whose very survival is not threatened by 'minor' events; consider, for example, the eruptions of violence in *Luke the Labourer*, Act I, Scene 2, in James Joyce's 'Counterparts' in *Dubliners*, and in Walter Brierley's *The Means Test Man*. Melodramatic styles of acting may even have been as close in some

But if we consider a range of cultural activities normally labelled 'popular', some doubt about this familiar line arises. For in a large number of cases, though in various ways, what seems an essential element in many popular cultural activities is precisely an experience by the audience of an actual or vicarious fear. The essential attraction of a circus, for example, surely lies in the acts which involve physical danger: the trapeze artist, lion tamer, high-wire acrobat, knife thrower, fire-eater, high diver and human cannon-ball are all experts in personal risk. It is not so much the spectacle or skill (the glittering girls on white stallions, the trick cyclist or juggler) that makes a circus memorable, as the tension in the pit of the stomach at the possibility of terrible failure or mistake; it is the high stakes that grip us, the lonely vulnerability of the performer in which, open-mouthed and edgily silent, we tinglingly participate. The same element seems present in that other great place of popular entertainment, the fair-ground; but there it is we ourselves who take the risks or simulate them: it is the Big Dipper and the giddy Big Wheel, the gyrating aerial torpedoes and the sickening slide of the helter-skelter that are the tempting high points — the other booths, those of skill or luck, seem a tame second-best, literally side-shows. In the fairground ghost train, as in its cinematic cousin the horror movie, we expose ourselves to the psychological frights without the physical risks; disaster movies, war movies and supernatural terror movies (*The Exorcist* and all its breed) exemplify the same pattern. In some sports, part of the thrill lies in the possibility of disaster: it is the flashing blue light of the ambulance in the centre of the speedway circuit that underpins the tension in the stadium. In its muted form, even gambling offers its own risks, of loss, failure, even disaster.

---

respects to working-class quotidian experience as, say, German expressionist film-acting was to the panic reactions visible in clips of the 1920s Stock Exchange crash: post-war hyperinflation had deeply affected the security of the German middle classes and one rather wonders just how 'exaggerated' those staring eyes seemed to someone actually facing imminent bankruptcy.

Much popular drama can also be viewed from this angle. The spectacular sensation scenes of Victorian melodrama (crashing trains, burning houses, sinking ships, avalanches and explosions) are the precursors of today's disaster movies; the melodramas of incantation anticipate *The Exorcist*; gothic melodramas are revived in the Hammer horror movies. And in domestic melodrama it is the persecuting pursuit of the helpless heroine by the malignant villain, the succession of 'hair's-breadth perils' engineered by the machinations of evil antagonists, that constitute the main content of the plot; the old serials of the children's matinee gave a cinematic half-life to these patterns of endlessly suspended peril.

In the standard accounts of melodrama this overwhelmingly obvious feature is, of course, acknowledged and dwelt upon; but it is then often subsumed under an account which puts emphasis rather upon the moral dichotomies that control the plot and characterisation: the stereotyping of Good and Evil characters, the 'poetic justice' of the (last-minute) triumph of the Sunday School virtues, the final evaporation of evil. Michael Booth's formulation can stand for many:

> Essentially, melodrama is a dream world inhabited by dream people and dream justice, offering audiences the fulfilment and satisfaction found only in dreams. An idealisation and simplification of the world of reality, it is in fact the world its audiences want but cannot get. Melodrama is therefore a dramatisation of this second world, an allegory of human experience dramatically ordered, as it should be rather than as it is. In this world life is uncomplicated, easy to understand, and immeasurably exciting. People are true to their surface appearances and always think and behave in a way these appearances dictate. One of the great appeals of this world is clarity: character, conduct, ethics, and situations are perfectly simple, and one always knows what the end will be, although the means may be temporarily obscure.

> The world of melodrama is thus a world of certainties where confusion, doubt, and perplexity are absent; a world of absolutes where virtue and vice coexist in pure whiteness and pure blackness; and a world of justice where after immense struggle and torment good triumphs over and punishes evil, and virtue receives tangible material rewards. The superiority of such a world over the entirely unsatisfactory everyday world hardly needs demonstration, and it is this romantic and escapist appeal that goes a long way to explain the enduring popularity of melodrama.

The last sentence particularly puzzles. A world of fear, terror, horror, violence, disaster, agony, of (in Booth's own phrasing) 'shootings, stranglings, hangings, poisonings, drownings, stabbings, suicides, explosions, conflagrations, avalanches, earthquakes, eruptions, ship-wrecks, trainwrecks, apparitions, tortured heroines, persecuted heroes and fearsome villains' seems a distinctly odd one to choose to escape *into* — even if it does constitute 'only a lengthy prelude to inevitable happiness'. James Smith somewhat similarly claims: 'poetic justice permits the free indulgence of our fears'.[10]

But neither critic seems to me very convincing about why a (working-class) audience should want this 'free indulgence' of its 'fears' in the first place. However, if we remember, and relate melodrama to, those other forms of popular entertainment in which considerations of 'poetic justice' or the 'triumph of good' seem irrelevant but where the element of fear also seems crucial, it may be suggested that it is the

---

10 Quotations arc taken from M. R. Booth, *English Melodrama* (London, 1965), p. 14 and J. L. Smith, *Melodrama* (London, 1973), p. 35. Cf. also F. Rahffl, *The World of Melodrama* (Pennsylvania, 1967). One might query other aspects of Booth's claims: I'm not sure that 'life', plots and situations in many melodramas are best described as 'uncomplicated, easy to understand' and 'perfectly simple', and it's worth noting that Smith devotes a chapter to the 'melodrama of defeat'.

experience of fear itself which is enjoyed rather than the long-suspended and last-minute 'catharsis'.

Various explanations of why a 'free indulgence in fears' might be welcome are, of course, possible: both Aristotle and Freud come to mind.[11] But if we place the experience of watching a melodrama within the surrounding experience of its audience, if we consider not just the internal trajectory of the plot itself (from initial, brief security through long and elaborate perils to re-established security) but also the over-arching 'before-and-after' of the whole performance for its audience (their life before they come to the theatre and after), it may be that a formulation from Strindberg (that sophisticated melodramatist) offers us a more interesting perspective. For if melodrama presents a dream-world, for much of its time that dream is a nightmare, and it is precisely as a nightmare that Strindberg describes his own *Dreamplay*:

> Sleep, the liberator, often appears as a torturer, but when the pain is at its worst, the sufferer wakes — and is thus reconciled with reality. For however agonising real life may be, at this moment, compared with the tormenting dream, it is a joy.

---

[11] Particularly Freud, though De Sade or Sacher-Masoch might be felt to be more appropriate. Freud's grandson playing his game of *Fort/Da* can serve as one analogue: the eighteenth-month-old boy negotiated the intermittent absences of his mother by displacing her disappearance onto those of his toy, throwing it away in order to have it returned; he thus played with his fear, turned his real insecurity into a reassuring game, a simulation and experiment. It may be that one function, and satisfaction, of much popular entertainment is to provide not so much an outlet for 'primitive' or 'exaggerated' emotions but rather a displacement, a way of coming to terms with actual fears by deliberately experiencing the emotions appropriate to vulnerability but in a controlled situation where a reassuring outcome is guaranteed. Obviously, the question of the relation between 'popular' and 'children's' forms of entertainment could be explored along these lines. Cf. S. Freud, *Beyond the Pleasure Principle*, Standard Edition, vol. 18, pp. 14f; cf. also the discussion of 'the drama of reassurance' in J. S. R. Goodlad, *A Sociology of Popular Drama* (London, 1971).

The escape, and fantasy, provided by melodrama may essentially have been not so much an escape into its world as an escape back from its world into the familiar world which, however insecure, irrational and hostile it might actually be, was then experienced by comparison as not as horrific and risk-laden as it might be. [12] Melodrama may have primarily presented for many of its audience not a (morally) 'superior' world but a decidedly worse and more physically frightening one in which to live. As the father, returning from a debtors' prison in *Luke the Labourer* (1826), put it: 'no man truly knows the blessings of his home but he who has been shut out from it'. There is, indeed, a parallel here to the actual experience of Samuel Bamford, almost the same year, who, having led a contingent at Peterloo, been tried for treason and imprisoned, finally returned home not to continued political agitation but to a settled domesticity, to a withdrawal into a privatised 'security'.[13]

The attractions of the 'normal', the familiar, may well be enhanced by a thrilling venture into adventure and that enhancement can have a deeply disabling effect politically. One might claim that, after coming out of a melodrama, it is the normal world which is made to seem more attractive — and, indeed, the internal structure of some melodramas rests not upon a final betterment of the initial situation but simply on the peculiar satisfaction of a return, more or less, to the *status quo ante*: it is the normal which becomes the normative ideal; that endorsement of 'normality' is at the root of conformism, of acquiescence, of ideology.

---

[12] The same pattern is, interestingly, discernible in that other Victorian dream/ nightmare, *Alice in Wonderland;* cf. e.g. Terry Eagleton, 'Alice and Anarchy', *New Blackfriars* , October, 1972.

[13] See my analysis of Bamford's *Passages in the Life of a Radical* in *Auto-biography and Class Consciousness*, unpublished PhD thesis, Cambridge 1974. Cf. too the middle-class response to the problem of casual labour, in terms of an emphasis on the 'housing question', in Jones, *Outcast London*, pt2.

Expertise and intimacy

Winton Tolles has suggested a general formula for melodrama: [14]

> Two human forces, A and B, are opposed to each other in a struggle to be decided by brains and chance . . . The action then leads the opposing forces through a series of artfully contrived crises, each more exciting and piquant than the last. Suspense is constantly present, and surprise occurs repeatedly as first A and then B gains the supremacy through the amazing influence of some apparently trivial factor. The most common device to throw the weight first on one side and then on the other is the shifting possession of some material object, preferably a letter. As the play develops the pace with which the commanding position changes accelerates, until in a whirlwind climax one force attains final victory.

This description could serve also as a formula for an exciting football match, and further elaborations of the parallel might be pursued: the black / white dichotomisation that governs the committed supporter's viewpoint, the low 'thrill-threshold' of the massed audience, the applicability of social-psychological interpretations in terms of escapism and release of emotions, etc. [15]

But I want here to emphasise two other aspects of spectator enjoyment of football which seem to be present in other

---

[14] Quoted in J. O. Bailey, *British Plays of the Nineteenth Century* (London, 1966), p. 33.

[15] For some interesting comments on football, cf. C. Critcher, 'Football and Cultural Value', *Working Papers in Cultural Studies*, 1 (Spring 1971). My term 'thrill-threshold' is adapted from Basil Bernstein's notion of differential 'guilt-thresholds' as between working and middle classes, cf. B. Bernstein, *Class, Codes and Control*, vol. 1 (London, 1971). Bernstein's work suggests an interesting approach to differences between 'popular' and 'middle-class' drama, in terms of both plot construction and character depiction, which cannot be elaborated here.

forms of popular culture. The first is that each man on the terraces is his own expert; he claims to know what the players, and referee, should do. Secondly, he often claims a curious kind of knowledge of the players as persons, almost an acquaintance-ship or friendship: characteristically, players in your own team are referred to by their first names and treated with the affectionately insulting disrespect reserved for close friends (consider for example the advice freely given by the crowd just behind a throw-in). The same two features can be observed at a local boxing or wrestling stadium and increasingly, perhaps, at county cricket grounds. It was the 'expertise' of the spectators which attracted Brecht to the model of the boxing match. But both the expertise and the intimacy seem to be, to a large extent, forms of self-pretence or semi-fantasy. Yet they both seem, in various ways, constitutive of the pleasure of much popular entertainment. The stand-up comedian in a working men's club, for example, is treated by the audience precisely as a kind of old acquaintance and the success of his act often depends upon his establishing a knowing intimacy with that audience (thereby enabling him, often, to get laughs from the fears and insecurities he knows they know he knows about).[16] The same is true of the pantomime dame and perhaps was true of the melodrama villain.

What is involved in all these cases is a complex interplay between the player and the role: the panto dame, or villain, makes no sense unless we simultaneously see through the character to the actor, and react 'exaggeratedly' to the personality of both character and performer — we are allowed to subvert the role and asked to make it live, in quite explicit ways (boos, hisses, 'Watch out behind you', etc.). [17]

---

[16] See the problems explored in John Osborne's *The Entertainer* and in Trevor Griffiths's *Comedians*. Cf. also the instructions to the actors in McGrath's *Fish in the Sea* and the note 'On the Play' in 7:84's *The Cheviot, the Stag and the Black Black Oil*. Brecht's 'alienation' acting devices are to some extent in continuity with this strand in popular styles.

[17] Cf. e.g. M. Booth (ed.), *English Plays of the Nineteenth Century*, vol. 5 (London,1976), p. 14.

The mark of the professionally assured club comic is that he *might* be a mate cracking jokes at the bar — but, subtly, isn't. The attraction of a Tommy Lawton or (though less so?) a Kevin Keegan is that you might have been playing instead of him (or so you half-think) — after all, you know as much about football as the experts, don't you. I suspect, though it would be difficult to show, that these elements are far less present in (what I think of as) characteristically 'middle-class' sport and entertainment: the crowd at Wimbledon may cheer Virginia Wade but they don't swear affectionately at her like an old friend, and though we may marvel at or envy Olivier's skill few of us really think of him as Larry.

This peculiar blend of real and pretended knowledge, real and fantasised acquaintanceship, can, obviously, be seen in other areas. For example, the fascination with the life style of 'stars' and royalty feeds upon a desire for anecdote, and 'inside knowledge' about the people behind the image, coupled with some sense that their extra-ordinariness is only a variation of ordinariness (so that I could, given the luck, turn out to be Tom Jones, Prince Charles or Georgie Best).[18] And obviously in the case, of, say, a star of melodrama this 'knowledge' deeply shapes the response to the 'terror' of the villain, since the audience both 'knows' the actor behind the role and claims an expertise in the techniques of his art: the sense of 'fear' is accompanied by, though not fully replaced by, an awareness of the illusory nature of its source.[19] A perhaps related aspect of this complex of attitudes is the urge to pass comments on a performance while it is in progress: the 'aside' and the 'ad-lib' are as much a feature of the audience's contribution as of the performer's in a club or even music hall act, while the louder and more physical expressions of opinion (catcalls, whistles and flying fruit) may be merely an appropriate and natural extension, to a

---

[18] Cf. e.g. R. Dyer, The Meaning of Tom Jones', *Working Papers in Cultural Studies*, 1 (Spring 1971).

[19] Cf. e.g. Dickens on 'the theatrical young gentleman's' expertise concerning melodramatic acting conventions, quoted in Booth, *English Melodrama*, p.198.

larger setting, of the *sotto voce* critical remark! Even if the audience kept silent during a favourite pantomime, as Thomas Dibdin's *Colombine* claimed in 1814, I presume they didn't sit mute during the five-minute scene changes.[20]

What is perhaps being displaced, or compensated for, here is a relative lack of kinds of knowledge elsewhere. Since the people who actually control our society are not known personally to many of us, and since the systematic nature of that control is itself difficult to grasp, [21] it may become important to assert an expertise and quasi-acquaintanceship in areas which at least masquerade as important.

If all we 'know' is what we actually know then most of us would have to acknowledge our almost complete ignorance and impotence as individuals in those areas of economic and political decision making that we uneasily know are 'beyond our ken' (to use that symptomatic phrase from a once popular radio programme), but which crucially affect us. Of course, the insecurity and impotence, the displacement of knowledge, that I've sketched have to be grasped as the effects of a whole system of control: ignorance of economics and politics, for example, is one product of an educational system which is institutionally geared to the 'failure' of most of its pupils (think, as a minor pointer, of the consternation of management if every shop steward had a degree in economics and business studies!). Royalty-adulation and strong personal feelings expressed about individual political leaders (Tony Benn or Maggie Thatcher) may be one way in which the economic and political system is rendered ideologically, i.e. 'safely', 'knowable' — as a music hall turn, derby match or melodrama.

---

[20] Cf. Booth, *English Plays*, vol. 5, p. 1, and *English Melodrama*, pp. 170-1.
[21] Cf. e.g. the analysis of The Controllers of British Industry' by M. Barratt-Brown in *Can the Workers Run Industry?*, ed. K. Coates (London 1968), and the list of Scottish landowners given by J. McEwen, 'Highland Land-lordism', in *The Red Paper on Scotland*, ed. Gordon Brown (Edinburgh, 1975)

If we now ask what today is the most 'popular' form of cultural activity (in at least a crudely head-counting sense of 'popular'), the obvious answer has to be 'watching TV'. Television, as a medium, has of course incorporated and modified various older forms of popular entertainment: we can see the adaptations in *The Good Old Days*, *Match of the Day*, *The Comedians*, the Christmas fare of pantomime and Billy Smart's Circus, and we can add the TV screening of horror movies. Westerns, Ealing comedies, cartoons, Chaplin and Whitehall farces.[22]

The significance of television can be explored in various ways — as, for example, the continual 'dramatisation' of society to itself or as the quintessential expression of the Society of the Spectacle.[23] What interests me here is how the experience of watching TV—with the family, in the normal domestic sitting-room—seems to combine and blend the elements of intimacy and expertise with something akin to escapism back into the *status quo,* an enhancement and endorsement of the 'normal'.

Variants on the elements of intimacy and expertise can be easily listed: the use of close-ups, the familiar faces of newscasters and actors, the sense of acquaintance with characters derived from regularly watching a long-running series, the personal interviews, the chat-shows, indeed the

---

22 Cf. e.g. *Football on Television*, ed. E. Buscombe, BFI Television Monograph 4 (London, 1975), and L. Masterman, 'Football on Television: Studying the Cup Final', *Screen Education*, 19 (Summer 1976). Dyer, in *Light Entertainment*, pp. 15—16, notes how different TV producers highlight or efface the element of dangerous risk in their handling of circus acts. On Ealing comedies cf. C. Barr, 'Projecting Britain and the British Character', *Screen* 15:1 (Spring 1974) and 15:2 (Summer 1974), and John Ellis, 'Made in Ealing', *Screen* 16:1 (Spring 1975).

23 Cf. e.g. Raymond Williams, *Television: Technology and Cultural Form* (London, 1974) and *Drama in a Dramatised Society* (Cambridge, 1975); Guy Debord, *La Societe du spectacle* (Paris, 1967).

whole notion of a 'television personality' — all these tend to induce a reaction similar to that in the relation between the football supporter and a local player: the same kind of advisory or derisory comments, friendly insults, back-chat, directed at the screen personality but also aired to the rest of the watching family, a shared acquaintanceship. And this goes with a kind of confirmation of 'knowledge' in other, and overlapping, areas: the critical or scoffing remarks about the 'experts' on *Match of the Day*, the family's interpolated anecdotes about the chat-show guests, the anticipatory answers during *University Challenge*. Much current affairs presentation depends upon an implicit insinuation that the viewer really knows a great deal more than he or she is likely to; some informative programmes seem to want to convey the impression to the viewer that their explanations of complex material are really directed at someone else, necessary only for some other viewer. Some quiz shows seem designed to test the contestant while implying that the audience already know the answers (on radio particularly, the appeal to the studio audience not to help the contestants high-lights this); the slow-motion replay of a catch or the use of telescopic lens during a Test Match cater to exactly this impression of viewer-expertise. [24] And of course the conversations about and derived from TV which occur between members of a watching family — and which seem an almost essential part of watching many kinds of programme — continue elsewhere, in the factory, at the shops, in the pub; television provides us all with both a common knowledge and an instant expertise. If once it might be claimed that there was no 'popular' museum or art gallery, philosophy or science, one might now suggest that television provides all these as well as a 'popular' (armchair) theatre. [25]

---

[24] One of the few useful analyses in this area is J. Tulloch, 'Gradgrind's Heirs: The Quiz and the Presentation of "Knowledge" by British Television', *Screen Education*, 19 (Summer 1976)

[25] Cf. Jean Vilar, 'Memorandum' (1960), translated in *Theatre Quarterly*, 23 (Autumn 1976), esp. p. 54.

But the kind of 'knowledge' that television offers is often moulded in precisely the form of 'knowing' personalities. A programme about Schoenberg, Einstein or John Ford presents a pictorial biography and anecdotes from old acquaintances but scarcely discusses the structure of a twelve-tone composition, the mathematics of relativity theory or the semiotics of film. A current affairs programme stages a polemical contest between 'well-known' economists rather than examining their economic theories; perhaps most obviously, political issues are transformed into clashes between individual politicians. What is offered in these forms of presentation is a peculiar form of mystified demystification: history is seen as made by actual men (and even, occasionally, women) but history (and art and science) is thereby reduced to biography and anecdote. *I Claudius* and *Panorama* link hands.[26] Perhaps the most consistently popular TV programme is the *News*, where personalisation and anecdote dominate most clearly. But the *News* also provides one of our contemporary equivalents of the melodrama sensation-scene: clips of earthquakes, train disasters, sinking ships, fires, explosions and shootings. And such 'actual' scenes are in continuity with the flow of other forms of natural and man-made violence presented to us fictionally.

'Violence on TV' has been endlessly examined,[27] but one facet not much discussed is that part of the acceptability or even attraction of 'violence' on TV may lie in the way its reality evaporates at the flick of a switch: the streets of

---

26 Cf. e.g. Stuart Hall, I. Connell and L. Curti, The "Unity" of Current Affairs Television', *Working Papers in Cultural Studies*, 9 (Spring 1976). This analysis has been criticised for, in effect, endorsing personalisation; cf. R. Coward, 'Class, "Culture" and Social Formation', *Screen*, 18:1 (Spring 1977); but when the controlling agents in an economic-political conflict are not generally known to the public a 'personalised' account can sometimes be revealing; cf. e.g. the analysis of GEC—AEI—EE in R. Jones and O. Marriott. *Anatomy of a Merger* (London, 1970).

27 A. Glucksmann, *Violence on the Screen*, BFI Education Department (London, 1971), summarises much of the debate. For a number of different perspectives-see the special issue of *Screen Education*, 20 (Autumn 1976), devoted to *The Sweeney*.

Kojak's New York or the Sweeney's London, the creepy terrors of Transylvanian castles, the napalmed villagers of Viet-Nam, all enhance the reassuring, solid presence of the surrounding sitting-room once the programme moves on or clicks off. Our own reality is intruded upon by another, frightening reality but one that we can render invisible, absent, by switching over or off and making a cup of tea. It's a very peculiar, and historically unprecedented, power to enjoy.

And while actually watching TV, the real home in which we watch operates as a norm which is curiously suspended but still present while another reality takes its place and takes place in it; the living-room becomes a palpable 'off-screen space' which continually reassures us against the lurking threats in the imaginary off-screen space of the horror movie. As we watch the violence and horrors of the world 'outside', brought 'inside' the home by the screen, the quiet and safety of that home becomes simultaneously an almost impossible ideal and an actual reality.[28] Television may provide an escapist avenue into a beautiful and impossible fantasy-world at times, but perhaps the main form of 'escapism' it offers is that repeated escape back into our own, safely familiar and familial living-room: whatever insecurities, fears or problems hover over our actual situation we are less at risk than in the world that glows through the darkness from the set in the corner.

It's possible to see why this structure of experience should be a particularly seductive one for an audience largely composed of people whose normal existence is constantly, if latently, under threat: in that situation the 'normal' is an

---

[28] To some extent, these two planes of reality can be seen operating within, say a horror movie, where the hero and heroine are nice and ordinary (i.e. acted more or less naturalistically) whereas the villains are melodramatic caricature The 1966 Hammer horror movie *Plague of the Zombies* includes an interesting use of a nightmare which arouses and then defeats expectations of a sequence being only a bad dream.

almost impossible ideal, rather precariously maintained, while the dangers threatening it (illness, unemployment, inexorable price rises) are both frighteningly real and yet invisible, lurking in an apparently different world that yet can intersect unexpectedly, inexplicably and disastrously with the familiar domestic world of everyday experience. To survive without neurotic anxiety one has then either to believe that the reality of those threats is an illusion which in the clear light of the next tomorrow will somehow evaporate or is a nightmare we can switch off when we wish — or one has to analyse, understand and defeat the sources of those threats. But to remove working-class insecurity in practice would mean collectively challenging and changing a whole society, an entire version of 'normality'.

Problems of popular political drama

With some exceptions, and for some obvious reasons, television itself has not been used to any great extent as a medium for (left-wing) 'political' drama. A great deal of politically motivated theatre this century has sought rather to use other forms of popular entertainment or to reproduce a popular format and setting. Thus we have seen agitational groups using melodramatic stereotyping for characters or adapting a *ceilidh* evening; others have staged rituals, festivals and pageants before 'mass' assemblies in sports stadiums; others have taken the circus or music hall as their model.

There are problems with these tactics, however, since what is taken over and adapted may be only the surface appeal of the models imitated. For example, the circus model may be seen in terms of spectacle and skills (lots of movement and colour, clowns and jugglers, Fellini-fashion), but what possible political use could be made of the crucial high-risk acts in terms of the vicarious fear involved? Or how could the actors in a play performed before 50,000 people achieve an intimacy with each spectator and how can the play itself become the affectionate target of self-confident and participatory 'expertise' from the audience?

More basically, if at the heart of much popular entertainment is a displacement of the experience of vulnerability and ignorance, and if political art seeks to present and analyse the determinants of that experience, how can this be achieved without destroying the very displacement which underpins the popular form being imitated?

There are, of course, various partial solutions to these difficulties, but they often raise other problems. An agit-prop drama may be used to precede political discussion or be designed as an intervention in a specific situation the audience is already involved in and knowledgeable about (a strike, an occupation, a campaign); or a political theatre group may be attached to and performing for a party whose members regard the group as, in some sense, their 'team'. But in these situations the effectiveness of the performance rests very much on a prior political *rapport* between performers and audience and thereby the dramatic activity itself can easily become a variant on the limited exercise of preaching to the already devout.

These are familiar points and have often been debated.[29] But given the massive popularity of television perhaps one crucial problem affecting all such tactics is the sense of cultural nostalgia that seems to permeate them: the utilisation of a largely superseded sub-text, model or

---

[29] *Theatre Quarterly,* 24 (Winter 1976), includes a useful discussion among various practitioners of many of these issues. One might extend the discussion of the use of nostalgic and media-based sub-texts by considering, say, *Sgt Pepper's Lonely Hearts' Club Band,* the albums of Pete Atkins and Clive James, or the work of the Liverpool Poets. For somewhat related problems in another medium, cf. E. and J. Cockcroft and J. Weber, *Towards a People Art: the Contemporary Mural Movement* (New York, 1977). It would be interesting to know if the National Front have any budding 'popular' dramatists.

medium. It is relatively easy to sketch a history of the communications media in terms of a repeated pattern of 'control lag': with each new technical development, the previously crucial medium becomes increasingly accessible to dominated groups, while the dominant group retains control over the new medium. When writing itself was the technically most advanced medium, only the ruling elite was literate; with the development of print a monopoly over the printing process was maintained while basic literacy became common; only when radio and television became the dominant media could oppositional groups operate with a fair degree of freedom in print — there are political as well as economic reasons for the relative ease with which an 'underground' press can flourish in the electronic era.[30]

There is perhaps a corresponding control lag in the cultural media; the battle for 'artistic freedom' — i.e. the struggle against censorship — seems to be regularly won only for modes of literary and artistic production which are already losing their social influence. It's not surprising that the major area of 'political aesthetics' is now film — a generation after the cinema ceased to be the dominant entertainment medium. The emergence of a breed of 'radical' dramatists may be precisely the sign that theatre is, in Truffaut's phrase, 'a fabulous anachronism'. The point can be made, very crudely, in terms of audience figures: after twelve years' work, one French 'popular theatre' group had been seen by about five million people; in the week I wrote this paper, 7.35 million watched the Monday *Coronation Street* episode and none of the 'top twenty' ratings was below 5 million — and that was a summer week. [31]

---

[30] Cf. Robin Murray and Tom Wengraf, The Political Economy of Communications'. *The Spokesman*, 5 (Summer 1970), and G. Murdock and P. Gold: 'For a Political Economy of Mass Communications', in *The Socialist Register 1973* (London, 1974), pp. 205-35.

[31] Cf. the chronology in *Theatre Quarterly* 23 (Autumn 1976), p. 60, concerning Vilar's Theatre National Populaire from 1951 to 1963, and *Financial Times*, 9 July 1977, p. 2. For various attempts at 'popular theatre'

This sense of 'lag' can extend to debates about political art even when the medium in question is television itself. Most considerations of such obviously political TV dramatists as Trevor Griffiths, Jim Alien, Loach and Garnett, have tended to focus on the one rather faded issue of 'naturalism'; criticism has concentrated on the limits of naturalism as a relapse into a pre-Brechtian mode or, more sophisticatedly, as a confirmation of the ideological positioning of the viewing subject.[32] But the comparison is thereby drawn mainly with other forms of theatre-drama rather than with other aspects of television itself, and it is then sometimes too easily presumed that 'naturalism' is the distinguishing mode of television, rather than recognising that many popular programmes on TV have little to do with naturalism and yet constitute a kind of, or utilise elements of, 'drama': situation comedies, quiz shows, *Morecambe and Wise* send-ups of naturalist theatre, even *News at Ten* itself. And, as Walter Benjamin recognised forty years ago, the nature of a technical medium may enforce a different awareness of what counts as 'art' — of what counts on television, for example, as 'drama'.

I suspect that the search for 'popular political drama' on television may itself be mainly a form of political as well as cultural nostalgia, and that political intervention in television has to operate not so much in terms of the 'drama' slots as in the field of 'Light Entertainment'. It could, after all, be argued that the radio programme which most memorably

---

in France, see E. Copferman, *Le Theatre populaire pourquoi?* (Paris, 1968), and P. Madral. *Le Theatre hors les murs* (Paris, 1969).

[32] Cf. the debate in *Screen:* C. MacCabe, 'Realism and the Cinema', 15:2 (Summer 1974), C. McArthur, 'Days of Hope', 16:4 (Winter 1975/6), C. MacCabe, 'Days of Hope: a Response', 17:1 (Spring 1976), C. MacCabe, 'Principles of Realism and Pleasure', 17:3 (Autumn 1976), R. Williams, 'A Lecture on Realism', 18:1 (Spring 1977). For other approaches, cf. Janet Wolff et al., 'Problems of Radical Drama: the Plays and Productions of Trevor Griffiths', in *Literature, Society and the Sociology of Literature, proceedings of a conference held at the University of Essex, July 1976* (University of Essex, 1977).

subverted the ideological complex of its period was *The Goon Show,* while, more recently, the Anti-Nazi League has had more success with 'Rock Against Racism' than with street-theatre.

But if we are to try to think beyond the familiar debate about 'naturalism', to try, for example, to carry over into television some of the political insights developed in the theatre by Brecht, then we seem to need a model of 'drama' which offers something different from a story, an anecdote, a reduction of issues to personalities or stereotypes, or merely a clash of perspectives. I can only, very tentatively, instance one TV programme which perhaps met some of these difficulties in a new way. Since I know of few references to it, it is worth outlining and commenting on as an example of an alternative model.[33]

Your Move

In 1967 Granada Television presented a programme called *Your Move.* It was basically a cross between a war game and an improvised play. A dozen members of a studio audience who had no professional connection with the educational system were assigned roles associated with the running of a school: Headmaster, Deputy Head, local NUT official, a teacher in Rank and File, PTA Chairman, Local Education Officer, School Governor, Conservative Councillor, etc. A situation was sketched by the programme's presenter: the Head is known to be against corporal punishment, but while he is away at a conference the Deputy Head severely canes some boys for trampling on flower beds; the Head returns and the boys' parents complain to him. The players then sat at a table and put earphones on.

[33] I once sketched an analysis of this programme in *Radical Arts,* ed. Bruce Birchall (London, 1968) —a publication which also includes some guerrilla theatre scripts of that vintage.

From then on there was no script and any player could make any 'move' they wished, subject to two limitations. First, the presenter controlled access to the microphones and earphones through which the moves were made, so a player had to request 'air-time', but it was up to the player making the move to decide who, among the other players, heard his move, though the studio audience and the viewers heard every move. Thus we could see what tactics and alliances were developing, how 'characters' were being elaborated or revealing them-selves, what moves were backfiring or cutting across others, etc., though the players remained in various states of ignorance about the overall state of play. The game quickly became complex and exciting while remaining intelligible and open-ended.

After about twenty minutes it was simply stopped and the studio audience was invited to comment on the various moves and the overall situation that had been reached — which by that stage included a parents' demonstration, a teachers' strike, an abortive arson attempt by some pupils, a deal concerning the promotion of the Deputy to be Head of a new comprehensive, engineered by the Tory councillor, etc.

The second limitation on moves is worth noting at this point: throughout, an 'expert' from the educational world advised the presenter if any move contravened definite regulations and laws or went against 'normal practice'; at the end of the game this expert's interventions were also subjected to scrutiny and critique by the audience and players.

This forgotten programme seems to me to have combined many of the elements that have preoccupied practitioners of political drama since Brecht. [34] It made explicit the notion of role-playing within an institution but subverted those roles,

---

[34] Cf. especially 'The Literalization of the Theatre', Brecht's notes to *The Threepenny Opera,* included in *Brecht on Theatre*, ed. J. Willett (London, 1973).

estranged them by assigning them to 'amateurs'. The educational apparatus itself was represented not as a fixed abstraction but as interacting agencies shaped by particular individuals' decisions within the constraints of others' decisions. The agents in the process were revealed as both subjects and objects of that process. The audience found itself thinking both within and above the flow of the game. The issue involved was an ordinary 'minor' crisis but we could see how major issues and powerful interests intersected with and converged upon it, how almost every move was overdetermined. No pre-given solution to the problems was imposed externally, by either an author or a political leadership who 'already knew' the 'answers'.

At the same time, the programme employed some of the features of 'popular' television: it allowed us access to a 'privileged' area of knowledge; it treated the ordinary person as competent and responsible in an unfamiliar field while allowing the rulings of the acknowledged expert to be queried; we could see 'ourselves' in the roles depicted and in the ordinary people playing them; it encouraged viewers at home to comment on both specific moves and general issues; we could participate vicariously in the risks of each move, with no script as safety-net or guarantee; it touched directly on something familiar but opened wider perspectives, clarified relations of power and control beyond our own experience of the educational system, as pupils or as parents of pupils; it brought us closer to the 'figures' who control events in an important sector without either offering stereo-typed caricatures or actual officials anxious to whitewash themselves; while departing from 'naturalism' it remained representational, but what was represented was not a story or anecdote so much as a structure of relations. The programme thereby offered an exercise in understanding rather than simply involvement in a plot or personalities; the 'real world' was suspended for a time but what re-placed it was a dramatic reality structurally homologous to a sector of that real world.

In various ways the format of *Your Move* could be used in connection with such issues as racism, discrimination against women, redundancy, abortion, unfair dismissal, a campaign for an adventure playground, a strike, eviction, an attempt to unseat an MP, a rent tribunal action, etc. etc. Viewed another way, the format lends itself to a specific dramatisation of crucial sectors of control and decision making; one could easily envisage an instructive version of *Your Move* for each of what Louis Althusser terms the 'Ideological State Apparatuses'.[35]

The basic format could also be adapted for use outside the television medium, as a form of 'live' drama, for example as prologue to a public meeting on some issue or as a form of rehearsal for, say, a factory occupation. The effect of such a game/drama should be to show both participants and spectators how a political situation can develop and how it can be controlled, what tactics and alliances are perhaps viable, what the possible consequences of certain moves might be. One of the various major reasons for in-security is ignorance and a sense of impotence, a timidity about trying to change a situation because one isn't, one thinks, equipped with the 'right' skills or knowledge to devise appropriate strategies and tactics against powerful forces felt to be waiting with pre-planned counter-moves ready. By taking part in as well as watching 'dramatic games' we might learn not only to feel more confident of our capacities in an insecure world but also begin to acquire some of the capacities necessary to change that world: a real knowledge of the structures of control and exploitation within which we live and practice in working effectively both within and against those structures.

A television programme like *Your Move* might be regarded as having little to do with 'theatre', but if we are searching for a 'popular theatre' we might take one more cue from Brecht.

---

[35] Cf. 'Ideology and the Ideological State Apparatuses', in L. Althusser, *Lenin and Philosophy* (London, 1971).

In the epilogue to *The Good Person of Setzuan* he invited the audience: 'You write the happy ending to the play! ' Perhaps it's time the 'audience' wrote the rest of the play as well, time the 'readers' became 'authors' themselves, time the process of 'reception' controlled and modified the conditions of 'production'.

*

TOWARDS POLITICAL DRAMA - NEXT MOVE ?

> I require no tombstone,
> but if you require one for me
> I wish it to be inscribed :
> He made suggestions. We
> accepted them.
> By such an inscription we should
> all be honoured.
>
> Bertold Brecht : *Epitaph*

Brecht's work in political theatre has left behind many suggestions and many problems. The root of his attempt to 'give the theatre a new function' can be crudely summarised as the attempt to weld together techniques from both Expressionism and historical drama, in such a way that the audience could grasp the 'characters' as both subjects and objects of the historical process. (*Notes to Threepenny Opera*) , thereby understanding their own task as simultaneously objects and subjects in a present historical process, demystifying the 'self-evident' givenness of history into a movement actively and evidently created by men (*Messingkauf Dialogues*). The basic technique he employed was to disclose the nature of theatre as 'work' , something made (*Poems on Theatre*) and the basic result he aimed at was that the audience should be activated to re-make their own history by overcoming the alienations of a capitalist work-process (*The Good Person of Setzuan*, especially the Epilogue).

Since Brecht, we have, of course, seen many attempts to work through and take further various aspects of his project, Wesker's *Trilogy* used fairly conventional techniques of characterisation, but by constructing his play across a period from 1936 to 1959 and by overlapping moments in the process of political experience of disillusionment in one family, with a 'horizontal' analysis of the beginnings of politicisation in another, connected with the first, he managed to convey some sense of the lived political experience of two decades of English working-class history. Peter Weiss's *The Investigation* stripped the stage of theatrical devices and forced the audience to stretch their minds round the evident horror of our tine, kept at mental bay and reduced to myth by sleight-of-memory: the sheer historical documented evidence of Auschwitz. But, as Peter Brook found in the Aldwych reading of the play, after twenty minutes or so the audience could even find atrocity boring : *Verfremdungseffekt ad absurdum.* The current atrocity of Vietnam is also a mundane boredom in the media. In trying to recreate that horror, Brook and the Aldwych company in *US* jerked every theatrical string, activating not intellectual comprehension but a felt sense of being comprehended, involved in that process, linked to Vietnam by cool attitudes rendered possible only by lies and the staleness of swamped responses; in *US* we were to be 'run over by the truth'. The truth is the whole and in *US* the whole was attempted.

But *US* drew on other theatre workers who have investigated closely more restricted areas. The work of Peter Cheeseman at Stoke-on-Trent, for example, tackling local history through the cooperative creation of the whole theatre team, was re-enacted in the cooperative production of *US*, the months of group-improvisation 'rehearsal'. Grotowski, erecting theatre into a total life for his actor-team, the whole truth felt through the bodies yet controlled by the scientifically surgical self-analysis of his Teatr Laboratorium *cum* monastery in Wroclaw .contributed less directly — though personally present for 10 days in the gestation stage — to the dramatic form of *US*, but his commitment and dedication gave a tenor to the final performance .

Yet in all these various attempts one blockage to what some would regard as the true direction for radical political theatre remains. Groups like Living Theatre, affected deeply by some aspects of the Grotowski mode, and even more, 'guerrilla theatre' groups, have reacted away from 'produced' professionalism towards, first, group improvisation in performance itself, and then at times spontaneous, active involvement of the audience also, breaking the final professional barrier. Experiments like Terry Hands' Theatre-go-Round presentations, which took literally Brecht's invitation to the *Setzuan* audience to re-write the ending to the play, have been surpassed, frenetically at times, towards a refusal to pre-structure any aspect of what could then invitingly be described as a 'happening'. The interaction here was to be two-fold - art/life categories (actor/audience distinctions) were to crumble, simultaneously redefining art as a form of ordinary, made, activity , and revealing everyday life as already a 'spectacle. '

Dissatisfaction , however, lingers over all these forms. May I suggest one possible way forward, not as spelling out the epitaph of other modes (even straight Stanislavski might have its appropriate place) but adding an alternative to the battery?

Conor Cruise O'Brien's play *Murderous Angels* recalls chess in its clarity and logic. Anticipating Debord, O'Brien long ago grasped the United Nations as a world-drama; in his play he turns the drama-politics relationship on its head: whereas the cold logic of the politics of disaster is diplomatically dressed and theatrically enshrined in the myth-creating professionalism of the corridors of power, O'Brien's play eschews most theatrical illusions and exposes the precise moves towards destruction The exactness of his presentation is not documentary but structural: . In seeing Hammarskjold, Lumumba, British business and Belgian imperialism portrayed as pawns between two Grand-Masters (off-stage), one is close to the deadly-clear diagrams of Strategic Air Command , the nuclear rationality of the war-game which dominates our historical consciousness; but one is also close, again, to Brecht: we see the made processes of history, we recognize in Hammarskjold the subject and object of decisions within a language-game he partly controlled and understood but which totally destroyed him. We 'sit and smoke in the theatre' as the limits of freedom actively constructed in our closed world kill a world-historical individual of our era.

This may seem remote from street theatres and their audiences. Mike Scott's recent work on Granada TV, claimed its massive audience (despairingly neglected or despised by most radicals) for encounters between tiny complaining individuals and the anonymous officials of 'their' local government (*On Site*). In concocting *Your Move* he transposed such encounters into a new dramatic mode. Since the programme, predictably, was not nationally net-worked at peak advertising hours, it probably needs description . For example, taking Education as a topic, Scott invited to the studio ordinary people not directly concerned in education, assigned them roles (Head, Vice-Head, Left-wing art teacher, PTA chairman, Local Education Officer, School Governor, Conservative Councillor, etc.) told them the official limits and conditions on their roles, the regulations actually governing the actions of people in such positions, and gave them a situation : the Head , opposed to corporal punishment, finds that the Vice-Head has caned two boys for trampling school flowerbeds — what is he to do? From that point, the direction of the drama/game depends on the specific moves chosen and made by the participants (via a Chairman). It is entirely up to them to seek allies, decide personal priorities, back down, ignore advice from other participants, etc.

What is specifically interesting is that (through the use of ear-phones and mikes on TV) any moves, while always being fully known by the audience, are known to other participants only at the discretion of those making the move. Moves may be 'public' (ear-phones off) or more or less private, known only to chosen allies, though affecting the context and process within which other participants' moves have to be made. The result is a genuine involvement in a situation without pre-structuring in which moves may backfire through ignorance (back to Aristotle). In this particular example, played on Granada TV, the provisional situation at the closure of the programme involved resignations, a teachers' strike, Ministry intervention, a PTA demonstration, plans for a new school, etc. The controlling structures of education within society were revealed as interacting agencies, not fixed abstractions, the processes were revealed as made history available for remaking .

Suggestions are best left open-ended; there is presumably no need to spell out in detail connections with previous modes (group-improvisation, ordinary people, ordinary life, subject/object, etc) but I will briefly point some applications: The form has limited political uses, but a Tenants' Association rent strike, a student campaign for participation, a case of eviction, or local agitation over anything from an adventure playground to street-traders, would all provide contexts in which such an interactive 'game' would be a viable contribution to the normal dreary and evasive public meeting. Its attraction is superficially that of courtroom drama, notoriously popular! — and by providing an involving situation for the casually interested it can help to counteract any creeping bureaucratisation within such a direct action group. The people at one end of the particular process inside one of the concentric circles of power could play out a dramatic re-enactment of the whole potential process, assume responsibilities actually wielded by the real incumbents of other positions in other circles; the understandings engendered and options played through would easily preface competent engagement with the real processes .

Two refinements: on TV an 'expert' was present to rule out moves which broke the existing laws and regulations governing education. In a public meeting such experts — the real incumbents (invited as audience members) — could be called to account (with explanations) for the legitimacy of the options adopted by their role-playing counterparts. Secondly: one assigned role in any situation (interestingly absent from Granada's presentations) might be that of press or TV reporter—also equipped with earphones—and thereby forced explicitly to rely on establishing 'contacts' — yet obliged to give a regular and 'full' newspaper account of the process in operation, which would of course influence the dispositions of other participants towards each other and the media...

One application of this idea of role-playing was seen when FACOP, which is a militant group of artists incensed at Covent Garden getting £1M. p.a. and living artists getting a mere £15,000 between them, and are therefore trying to screw more bread out of the Arts Council, planning to go into an official Arts Council meeting to which they weren't invited, spent up to a fortnight with a theatre director rehearsing the confrontation they were after — anticipating the bureaucrats' moves and their counter-moves — marking out ways they might get sidetracked or absorbed from their purpose, and building up their own confidence individually and as a group .

The suggestion rests. Your move .

*

RAISONS DES TEXTES

by Editions du CEAL

[an imaginary book]

This latest collective and anonymous product of the now notorious 'Cercle d'Ecole Abnormale des Lettres' is a strange, even unnerving work, yet despite its peculiarities and its undermining effect upon the reader it seems to offer, in an intricate and labyrinthine way, an argument that carries a certain conviction. Not that the argument is pellucid or even easily apparent. Far from it.

I was reminded, as I persevered with its elliptical organisation and opaque style, of an occasion shortly after the second world war, when a group of Anglo-American philosophers arranged a conference with what they foolishly took to be their Parisian counterparts, in the hope of exchanging enlightenment on that tricky but topical term 'Freedom'. The opening paper, boldly but simply entitled '*La Liberté*' was given, I believe, by Gabriel Marcel. An hour of passionately earnest French from Marcel was followed by a series of wholly uncomprehending questions from the Anglo-Saxons. Communication clearly had not been achieved. Finally, in a desperate response to one bewildered probe from an Oxford don who had yet again requested a lucid definition of 'Liberty', Marcel threw up his hands and exclaimed: 'If I had a piano I could *play* it!' The Anglo-Saxons remained non-plussed.

This book is, I suspect, the score for some unplayable piece on an unimaginable variation of Marcel's piano. Its themes intertwine with such almost uncontrolled complexity that I doubt if I have deciphered more than a minimum of its melodies. But let me attempt my own faltering rendition.

One key lurks in the title. As I hear it, *Raisons des textes* echoes *raisons d'état* and this is certainly a work concerned with politics. But if we try a translation as, say, 'Textual Reasons', we are alerted to the predominant procedure of the book: the analysis of how texts deploy or embed particular modes of reasoning. Prominent among the texts chosen are various forms of 'detective' narrative, in a section sub-titled *Raisons détectifs*. But the opening part of the book seems to concentrate on two other usages of *raison*, the notion of reaching *l'âge de raison* ('years of discretion') and what in English we would call 'taking the law into one's own hands' (*se faire raison à soi-même*). The actual text begins abruptly, bafflingly:

> Does not the true character of each epoch come alive in its children? A child has much to learn before it can pretend. Full citizenship belongs to men both of whose parents were citizens, and they are inscribed on the list with their fellow demesmen when they are eighteen years old. When they are being registered, the members of the deme vote under oath first on whether they appear to have reached the legal age, and if they do not, they are returned to the status of children, and secondly on whether a man is free and born as the laws prescribe. If they decide that he is not free, he appeals to the dikasterion, while the demesmen select five of their number as accusers; if it is decided that he has no right to be registered as a citizen, the city sells him into slavery.

From the third sentence on, it is easy to recognise that we are faced with a quotation from Aristotle's *Athenian Constitution* (XLII). But the initial two sentences might puzzle us. The first is, however, another quotation, part of Karl Marx's embarrassingly *naif* response to the problem he formulates in the *Grundrisse*:

> the difficulty lies not in understanding that the Greek arts and epic are bound up with certain forms of social development. The difficulty is that they still afford us artistic pleasure and that in a certain respect they count as a norm and as an unattainable model.

The second sentence comes, I'm told, from Wittgenstein, but its source is perhaps less important than its placing here, suggesting that, somehow, it links Marx's problem with Aristotle's account of the constitution of Athens. But how?

The next paragraph offers some definite clues. Again, the whole extended paragraph is made up of quotations, rather bewilderingly interlacing Aristotle's *Rhetoric* and *Poetics* with the closing pages of Wittgenstein's *Philosophical Investigations.* The text itself disdains to identify the quotations beyond marking transitions with a slash, thus:

> The Emotions are all those feelings that so change men as to affect their judgements. Such are anger, pity, fear. / Imitation is natural to man from childhood; he is the most imitative creature in the world, and learns at first by imitation. / Take for instance the emotion of anger: here we must discover what the state of mind of angry people is, who the people are with whom they usually get angry, and on what grounds they get angry with them. Unless we know all three, we shall be unable to arouse anger in any one. / Is there such a thing as 'expert judgement' about the genuineness of expressions of feeling? Even here there are those whose judgement is 'better' and those whose judgement is 'worse'. / Can one learn this knowledge? Yes; some can. Can someone else be a man's teacher in this? Certainly. What one acquires here is not a technique; one learns correct judgement. / Ask yourself: how does a man learn to get a 'nose' for something? And how can this nose be used? / He who feels the emotions to be described will be the most convincing; distress and anger, for instance, are

portrayed most truthfully by one who is feeling them at the moment. / It is not right to pervert the judge by moving him to anger, envy, pity — one might as well warp a carpenter's rule before using it. / Tragedy is an imitation not only of a complete action, but also of incidents arousing pity and fear. Such incidents have the very greatest effect on the mind when they occur unexpectedly and at the same time in consequence of one another. / Fear sets us thinking what can be done. Consequently, when it is advisable that the audience should be frightened, the orator must make them feel that they really are in danger of something, pointing out that it has happened to others who were stronger than they are, and is happening, or has happened to people like themselves, at the hands of unexpected people, in an unexpected form, and at an unexpected time. / All terrible things are more terrible if they give us no chance of retrieving a blunder. / There might actually occur a case where we should say: 'This man believes he is pretending.' / Rhetoric is an offshoot of dialectic and also of ethical studies. Ethical studies may fairly be called political; and for this reason rhetoric pretends to be political science. / The older poets make their protagonists discourse like statesmen, and the moderns like rhetoricians. / When children play at trains their game is connected with their knowledge of trains. It would nevertheless be possible for the children of a tribe unacquainted with trains to learn this game from others, and to play it without knowing that it was copied from anything. One might say that the game did not make the same sense to them as to us.

I'm not convinced that these elliptical transitions achieve anything other than compression, but the task of disentangling the juxtapositions does force one to think, to come to one's own conclusions as to what line of argument is being implied, while at the same time driving one back to the quoted texts themselves, disengaging those texts from the uses made of them.

The irritation this causes is at least accompanied by a certain freshness, a relief from the tedious familiarity of unresolvable arguments about the relation between the *Rhetoric* and the *Poetics*. Moreover, that placing together of, for example, *Rhetoric* 1356a, *Poetics* 1450b and Wittgenstein's laconic remarks reminds us that not only our own reactions to 'Greek tragedy' but also Aristotle's are situated within a moving history, as Marx had recognised; furthermore, in awarding undifferentiated textual status to quotations from all three thinkers, *Raisons des textes* relativises the authority of each epoch against the others.

Clearly, however, the main insinuation of these opening paragraphs is that Greek tragedy is somehow linked to the assumption and exercise of adult citizenship in Athenian society, as perhaps the familiar pastimes of children in our society are associated with their eventual achievement of adult status. Pretence and imitation, performance and judgement, are being elliptically correlated for us. Though the precise reason for the enigmatic inclusion of the last entry in *Philosophical Investigations* II, xi, next to that famous use of *hamartia* ('retrieving a blunder') eludes me, unless 'believing that one is pretending' is somehow the most terrible mistake of all, the tragic error.

It is judgement that provides the next main thread. We are given two parallel columns, dividing the page. The left-hand quotes, in full, chapters LXIII to LXV of the *Constitution of Athens*, detailing the elaborately complicated process by which the *dikastoi* ('jurors') were allocated to particular law-courts each day. The right-hand column contains a selection of the meagre textual evidence that survives concerning the judging process at the dramatic festivals.

What emerges from this implied comparison is that in both courts of justice and dramatic contest the judging was entrusted to citizens assigned to their role, as far as possible, by lot. The Athenians even devised an elaborate 'randomiser' in the form of an 'allotment machine' (a diagram of which enlivens the text here) to distribute jurors between courts and cases.

These parallel passages are then suddenly succeeded by a single quotation in English:

> The sheriffs, instead of suffering the Jury to be struck at the places where the book of the Freeholders is kept, and by the officers to whom that care ordinarily falls, sent for the books from the office and took the task upon themselves . . It is very obvious to every person who casts his eye over the lists, that it consists of a most extraordinary assemblage, king's tradesmen, contractors, and persons labouring under every kind of bias and influence.

I myself had to wait until I was much further into the book before I was confidently able to identify the source here: William Godwin's *Cursory Strictures on the Charge Delivered by Lord Chief Justice Eyre*—an article published in *The Morning Chronicle*, 21 October 1794, criticising the 'charge' to the deliberately 'packed' Grand Jury in the trial for 'High Treason' of the radicals Thomas Hardy, Home Tooke, John Thelwall, and Thomas Holcroft.

The next of these abruptly juxtaposed quotations was easier to trace:

> 6. *The uneven development of material production relative to, e.g. artistic development.* In general, the concept of progress not to be conceived in the usual abstractness. Modern art, etc. This disproportion not as important or so difficult to grasp as within practical-social relations themselves. E.g. the relation of education . . But the really difficult point to discuss here is how the relations of production develop unevenly as legal relations.

7. *The point of departure obviously from the natural characteristic*; subjectively and objectively. Tribes, races, etc.

These jottings are of 'points to be mentioned here and not forgotten' at the end of Marx's *Notebook 17* (the *Introduction* to the *Grundrisse*). They immediately precede the notorious passage on Greek art. The authors of *Raisons des textes* obviously think the jottings are intimately related to that passage. Their own link, however, is made more immediately with the final two words 'Tribes, races', for they follow the Marx quotation with a series of fragmentary extracts from a range of sources, all describing the 'reforms' of Cleisthenes in 508 BC. For example:

> The people had taken control of affairs, and Cleisthenes was their leader and champion of the people . . He first divided all the citizens into ten tribes instead of the earlier four, with the aim of mixing them together so that more might share control of the State . . He divided Attica into thirty sections, using the *demes* as the basic unit; ten of the sections were in the City area, ten around the coast, and ten inland. He called these sections *trittues*, and placed three into each tribe by lot, one from each geographical area. He made fellow demesmen of those living in each *deme* so that they would not reveal the new citizens by using a man's father's name, but would use his *deme* in addressing him. Hence the Athenians use their *demes* as part of their names . . These changes made the constitution much more democratic than it had been under Solon.

One could add, of course, that Cleisthenes' reshaping of Athenian social identity made things a great deal more complicated as well! I suspect that any Parliamentary Boundaries Commission faced with a proposal along Cleisthenes' lines would promptly ignore it as impractical.

Yet there is a genuine simplicity underlying this surface complexity: tribal, kinship and even regional interest-groups were replaced by constituencies whose only real definition was one of electoral equality. Even the apparent basis of the *demes* (wards) in geographical neighbourhoods had little effective weight, since a change of residential location did not modify one's deme-membership As one distinguished historian has commented:

> If a man still belonged to his deme, no matter where he lived, the neighbourhood principle was no longer in full force, but neither had it been replaced by new bonds of kinship. If anything now counted beside the local principle, it was the individual citizen whose political activity had sometimes few ties left with any larger groups.

In other words, what we can see in the reforms of Cleisthenes is the creation of that curious (even etymologically paradoxical) unit: the political individual.

Raisons des textes concludes this selection of extracts on the reforms of 508 BC with a single Greek word: ισονομια — *isonomia* — which is perhaps not quite translatable. It indicates not only 'equality at law' or equal access to law, but also equal rights over the law, an equal say in determining what 'the law' is. In a sense which escapes even the literal meaning of our colloquialism, each Athenian citizen 'took the law into his own hands'.

In the kind of textual gesture one is now prepared for, that single glowing word *isonomia* is immediately followed by a news item from *Le Monde*, concerning the activities of the Communist Mayor of a small town in France who personally led an illegal attack on an immigrant workers' hostel. No doubt different French readers will draw their own conclusions from this particular juxtaposition!

The same could be said of the next abrupt switch from classical to contemporary sources. Two brief extracts, from Aristotle and Plutarch, offer interestingly divergent summaries of Solon's reforms (c. 594 BC):

> The following seem to be the three most popular features of Solon's constitution: first and most important, that nobody might borrow money on the security of anyone's freedom; secondly, that anyone might seek redress on behalf of those who were wronged; thirdly, the feature which is said to have contributed most to the strength of the democracy, the right of appeal to the *dikasterion*, for when the people have the right to vote in the courts they control the constitution . . . Some think that Solon made his laws obscure deliberately, to give the people the power of decision. This is not likely; the obscurity arises rather from the impossibility of including the best solution for every instance in a general provision.

> The rest of the citizen body were known as *thetes*; they were not entitled to hold office and their only political function consisted in sitting in the Assembly or on a jury. This latter privilege appeared at first to be worth very little, but later became extremely important, because the majority of disputes were finally settled before a jury. Even in those cases which Solon placed under the jurisdiction of the magistrates, he also allowed the right of appeal to the popular court. He is said also to have framed the laws in obscure and contradictory terms and to have done this deliberately so as to increase the power of the popular courts. In consequence, since the parties to a dispute were unable to settle it according to the letter of the law, they were constantly obliged to resort to the juries and lay every disagreement before them, so that in a sense the jurors became the arbiters of the laws.

These two quotations are followed, quite impishly, by a chart showing the social origins, educational background, and estimated average earnings of the legal profession in France. In the spirit of this procedure, but with a slightly different point in mind, I would myself have also included an extract from, say, the small print in a deed of conveyance.

Here the text of *Raisons* again divides, and in parallel columns we are offered: (a) accounts of the various formal stages in a Greek trial; and (b) an extremely truncated version of Aeschylus, *Eumenides*, lines 408-753. Readers familiar with, for example, A. J. Podlecki's *The Political Background of Aeschylean Tragedy* will need no reminding that this confrontation between Athena and the Furies at Orestes' trial does indeed follow, in broad terms, the actual processes of a Greek court.

What the authors of *Raisons* make insufficiently clear by their method of simple parallelism is that Greek legal procedures differed considerably, depending on the nature of the case and of the court to which it was referred. The procedure in a homicide case before the Areopagus court would not have been identical to, say, a theft case heard before an ordinary dikasterion. In addition, our sources for reconstructing Greek legal modes make it clear that, as one would expect, practices current in the early fifth century cannot be assimilated to those obtaining in the late fourth. For example, even the passage from Aristotle concerning Solon's reforms clearly reads later developments back into Solon's time — and it is even worth reminding ourselves here, incidentally, that Plutarch was writing some 600 years after the events re-counted.

However, within the context of what I see as the emerging argument of the book, the point is appropriately and adequately, though not exactly, made: that Aeschylus embeds within his play a formal process of trial which, as it were, recapitulates the process which the whole audience is also following, on two levels: they too are passing judgement both on Orestes and on the play itself, and of course — as George Thomson argued long ago — the whole Oresteian trilogy deals with the transition from modes of justice associated with kinship (vengeance, vendetta) to judicial forms of law developed in the city-state democracy, the polis. In passing judgement upon this trilogy the assembled audience is judging a dramatic representation of part of the development whereby they came to be 'judges' themselves.

One can see how some at least of the themes in this book are harmonizing at this point. But a perhaps unexpected variation intervenes here. Three words, in Greek, spread themselves across the page:

CHOEPHOROI ELECTRA ELECTRA

The point of so emphatically isolating the titles of the three dramatisations of the avenging of Agamemnon's murder — by Aeschylus, Sophocles and Euripides (though omitting Euripides' further version in the *Orestes*)—is indicated in the quotation from the *Poetics* that follows:

> Tragedy is an imitation not of persons but of actions and of life, of happiness and misery. All human happiness or misery takes the form of action; the end for which we live is a certain kind of activity, not a quality. Character gives us qualities, but it is actions that are happy or the reverse. In a play accordingly they do not act in order to portray the characters; they include the characters for the sake of the action. So that it is the action and the shape of the action that is the end and purpose of tragedy; and the end is, as always, the chief thing. Besides, a tragedy is impossible without an action, but there may be one without characters. The tragedies of most of the moderns are characterless — a defect common among poets of all kinds.

The fuller implications of placing these titles and this passage here is signalled rather startlingly by what immediately follows: a full-page reproduction of a photograph of a young child who is obviously near to death from starvation. Across the photograph is a headline, '*Famine in Somalia*', and printed at the foot of the picture is the address of a voluntary aid agency. The photograph is taken from a popular French magazine, and is the equivalent of our familiar Oxfam posters. Faced with this, it is clearly intended that the reader should pause.

*

Let me now do so, in order to make some general comments, prompted by this particular concatenation, concerning the overall 'argument' of the book thus far — as I reconstruct it.

Aristotle, in the *Poetics*, emphasises that once a dramatist has chosen his 'story' he should reduce it to the essential elements of its *structure*, its *dramatic shape*. After that he can fill up the necessary 'positions' in the 'plot' with suitable 'characters'. But the 'tragedy' resides in the structure of events, the chain of episodes, the diagram of forces, not in the characterisation of the agents in the action.

For example, we can see Sophocles solving some of the technical dramatic problems he had inherited from Aeschylus (and, probably, Euripides) in his introduction of a sister for Electra into his re-working of the Electra situation: the 'personality' he attributes to Crysothemis is subordinate to, is indeed subject to, the considerations of plotting and sequence of 'effects' which constitute the core of his *Electra*. It is the tragic situation that demands our response, not the secondary feature that it is Electra's situation. But the very fact that Sophocles calls his play *Electra* indicates a certain tilting of an older balance: a 'character' is always essential for a 'situation' (an Oedipal complex requires someone to be

Oedipus) but with Sophocles and even more with Euripides we feel that the character, the personality, looms larger than it did in Aeschylus, begins even to loom larger than the persona, the mask.

Here we might note that a post-Romantic sensibility — i.e. anyone attuned to the pre-suppositions of the Romantic lyric or realist novel — has great difficulty in grasping the basic movement of, say, *The Libation Bearers* (*Choephoroi*) where 'character' is assumed with function in the process of the curse: 'Orestes' summons up and is in part 'replaced by' the 'character' of the dead Agamemnon — the great (transfiguration) scene at the tomb which gives the play its first focus and title.

One might say that after Wordsworth's *Preface* to the *Lyrical Ballads* (a title which itself indicates the threshold of a new outlook), we have sought the situation in literature for the sake of the emotion, rather than grasped through the nature of the emotion the nature of the situation. An instance of the kind of problem a Wordsworthian approach generates might be our response to Thomas Hardy's poems of 1912-13: we tend to read 'through' them to the autobiographical situation which prompted them, rather than grasp in the reading of the poems themselves the X-ray Hardy offers us of a kind of situation, a *type* of a whole relationship. Some audiences have a similar difficulty with Samuel Beckett's plays, for example *Footfalls* or *That Time*.

It's fairly clear, however, from Aristotle's *Poetics*, that the kind of response familiar to a Greek audience was balanced the other way: it is the dramatist's ability to reveal to us the basic pattern of a situation that constitutes his value. And that value is fundamentally political, since it is the 'political situation' that we are summoned to grasp, to understand, to appreciate: the situation of the *polis*.

But given this balance between situation and character, between dramatic structure and its agents, it can be suggested that a certain capacity for 'emotional' reaction was available to an Athenian assembly or audience in a way which we characteristically find it hard to summon up today.

Faced with a real 'tragic' situation which does not involve those known personally to us, those near to us or those of our own 'kin', we can remain unmoved, whatever the scale of the 'tragedy'. Reading our morning papers about yet another famine or flood disaster, massacre or 'outrage', we tend to need the stimulus of personalised presentation — the hollow cheeks of the starving child on the Oxfam leaflet — before we react with what we feel to be the appropriate feelings.

Yet 'pity' or even 'anger' may be deeply *in*appropriate for any effective action: feelings diminish fast, the basic situation remains. It is not merely, or only, particularly sharply vivid events that demand our political judgement and verdict, but rather *the whole structure of relations* which shapes and generates those events. Those relations are not 'personal' relations in the first instance, though it may be *through* recognising the sufferings of individuals that we are brought to recognise the shape of the whole.

Recognition is not, however, enough. At the dramatic centre of a Greek tragedy is a moment of *anagnorisis* — of re-cognition, of seeing-as, of the acquisition of knowledge, but a peculiar and unwelcome kind of self-knowledge. When that moment was also constituted as a moment of *peripeteia* — of a reversal of direction, a pivot of action — the lesson of the drama was most valued: the aim, the end, of the dramatist was to show process changing into praxis.

Now, to return to *Raisons des textes*, the point that the authors from C.E.A.L. seem to be suggesting is that the essential function of Greek drama was precisely to provide a political education for the citizens of democratic Athens, a form of public training in the nature of decision-making, a representation of what is involved in correct and incorrect judgement both within and about certain kinds of critical political situation.

By selecting passages from the sources which present Athenian citizens as 'judges', as members of the courts which (according to Plutarch) became the crucial decision-making centres in the internal life of the *polis*, we are reminded that each citizen had the responsibility for deciding the laws by which he was governed (*isonomia*).

Yet this needs, I think, qualification. The collective 'judges' of the courts comprised very large numbers of the citizen body: each 'jury' was probably 200 or more, and up to 6,000 citizens could be involved in deciding an important case. But one could only sit in the courts after reaching the age of thirty, though one could attend the Assembly, and vote, from the age of eighteen.

In other words, from eighteen to thirty the Athenian citizen was still an apprentice 'politician', still learning to qualify as a fully responsible member of the *polis*—and one (perhaps *the*) crucial element in that qualifying process is to be located in the attendance (perhaps even compulsory for some categories—the *ephebes*) at the dramas, which were themselves (so it is implied by the passages from Aristotle) concerned with exploring and presenting the various ways in which 'emotions' could sway and warp correct judgement.

What the plays essentially re-present are situations, within which someone—normally in authority—makes an incorrect judgement, while the audience is prompted not so much to make a correct judgement themselves as to see why the character's judgement was incorrect, what it led to and why. In that sense, the plays offer a negative training. And this is certainly consonant with that interesting feature of the legal procedures which is highlighted in the extracts we are offered: the interchangeability of all (adult, male, free, qualified) citizens, implied and secured in the apportioning of jurors by lot.

It is not the 'individual' characters or qualities of the jurors that are important, nor are the merits of the individual in each case to be judged; it is the *case itself* that has to be judged, impartially, without the jurors being affected by 'inappropriate' emotions. There is, of course, considerable difficulty even in formulating this requirement, since 'emotions' and the individual characteristics of the litigants would, obviously, play a role in any specific actual situation. But just as each citizen is inter-changeable, so each law-making decision has to be applicable to every citizen, in principle.

What is ultimately at stake in the Athenian courts is a decision as to what is 'correct' or 'incorrect' for the *polis*, i.e. for the citizens as a whole. It is this which is the fundamental meaning of *isonomia*. But such collective decision-making requires a very considerable degree of *individual responsibility*: each juror decides the law in deciding each case (existing 'laws' were regarded as only part of the 'evidence' in a case, not as determining rules) — and the jurors were not even allowed to discuss the case together before voting on a verdict.

An argument along these lines is, I think, apparent in the particular selection of quotations that *Raisons des textes* offers. There are problems to which I want to return, but an important point needs to be made here concerning the relation between this 'argument' and the mode in which it is presented by the C.E.A.L. authors. From 378 BC all 'evidence' in an Athenian court had to be presented in a written form; it was then read out during the hearing by the 'clerk of the court' (to use the English term). A sharp formal differentiation was thereby made between the evidence and what was said *about* that evidence by the interested parties — a distinction echoed in Aristotle's differentiation between persuasion which can be produced by the art of the orator and persuasion which cannot (1355b 35).

What the authors of *Raisons* have apparently attempted to do is simply to provide 'evidence' while eschewing the 'art of the orator' entirely. By selecting, arranging and juxtaposing quotations from various sources they are, of course, using a mode of 'persuasion', but they have deliberately refrained from arguing about that evidence and from making explicit any conclusions they themselves might draw from it.

But this procedure itself has further implications. Presumably, for example, they are aware that Aristotle himself maintains — in the very *Rhetoric* from which they quote so often — that:

> Persuasion is achieved by the speaker's personal character when the speech is so spoken as to make us think him credible. We believe good men more readily than others . . It is not true . . that the personal goodness revealed by the speaker contributes nothing to his power of persuasion; on the contrary, his character may almost be called the most effective means of persuasion he possesses.

But in *not* citing this passage, in ignoring its relevance to what seems to be their general case, are they implying that their 'evidence' is deliberately 'slanted', or that they are — perhaps more legitimately — constructing an 'ideal' case which may not have actually obtained, or at least no longer obtained by the time Aristotle wrote?

Perhaps, however, one has to acknowledge an even more drastic implication. Anyone even reasonably familiar with the sources they extract from will recognise that a quite different selection could have been made — and therefore rather different conclusions could be drawn, suggested. But in fact *they* draw no conclusions at all! At most, they prompt the reader to see connections; in particular, by their sudden inclusion of such passages as those from Wittgenstein, Godwin and *Le Monde* they invite an application of this body of material to issues and concerns which are not, in any direct sense, 'relevant' to a discussion of fifth-century BC legal or dramatic practice at all! It is, in any case, the reader who draws any 'conclusions' or 'parallels' — and in doing so either does or does not connect this material with the current concerns of the reader.

An instance of this would be my own response to that particular juxtaposition of three titles of Greek plays, a passage from the *Poetics*, and the photo of a starving child: the argument I outlined earlier is my responsibility, not theirs. But then, in a rather curious way, aren't *I* 'answering' Marx's question concerning the continuing relevance of Greek art and drama—the problem implied in the very first quotation in *Raisons des textes*?

There is a further turn to this spiral the text sets up, but for the moment let me return to the text itself. If I have coherently grasped the overall direction of the implied argument so far, it is clear that a problem now looms. Is there any 'evidence' *within* the plays themselves that they could have operated as modes of 'political education' in the way *Raisons* (or, more strictly, I myself!) has implied—and, more intriguingly, how could *Raisons* present any such case without itself finally resorting to some form of critical commentary, or oratorical persuasion?

*

The C.E.A.L. authors 'solve' this dilemma with a certain impudent neatness. They simply print a number of Greek plays—but not in full! By a skilful process of cutting and editorial stitching they present us with extremely condensed versions of selected plays, which not only retain the movement and shape of the originals but are actually composed entirely of authentic lines and phrases—yet the resulting texts are only between 150 and 250 lines long. (In addition, they italicise words or phrases, surely a *sotto voce* rhetoric?) Because, however, the reader already knows the originals, the effect is almost as powerful as reading the whole: as we read we simply 'supply' what is missing.

I remember once seeing a performance of a fifteen-minute 'version' of *King Lear*: the impact was quite overwhelming, as if the whole of the play had actually been compressed and intensified into that brief time. The impact of these cut-down versions of the Greek dramas is somewhat similar. In a sense, Aristotle's advice to prospective play-wrights has been reversed: starting from the whole text of the play, the authors have here 'reduced' it back to what it might have been in an earlier stage of its composition, the 'essential shape of its action' according to Aristotle's notions.

At the same time, their procedure reminds us that, in many respects, contemporary critical writing does, in effect, do the same. A critical essay on a novel, for example, often deploys quotations precisely in such a way as to create an 'edited version' of the whole novel, a selective reading of linked passages which then substitute for the whole. And, of course, the selection or editing is made in the light of a (prior) critical 'case' — just as the editing process which produces any actual performance-text today results from the interpretative decisions of the director and producer. The composite production of *The Greeks* by the Royal Shakespeare Company some time ago is a case in point.

In all, seven Greek plays are presented in this way in *Raisons*, arranged in two groups: Aeschylus, *The Suppliants*, Sophocles, *Antigone* and *Oedipus Tyrannos*, Euripides, *Bacchae*, in one group, and three plays by Euripides in another: *Women of Troy*, *Helen* and *Ion*. It is worth outlining what seems to be the basis for this compressed repertoire.

The first group are obviously related to the general theme of law. In *The Suppliants* we are given a drama about the relations and conflicts between laws based on kinship (parental authority in particular), laws decided by the citizen body (the norms of behaviour which the Suppliants apparently agree to accept in seeking sanctuary), and laws derived from the gods. *Raisons*' version of the *Antigone* emphasises not the Hegelian contrast of two 'absolutes' but rather the conflict between Creon's imposition of his own authority, as political leader, and the final appeal — which the broken Creon eventually has to make — to the decisions of the whole citizenry, represented by the Chorus. In this version it is Creon's line at 1099 which becomes the pivotal moment of peripeteia and anagnorisis:

> What must I do? Speak, and I shall obey.

Creon has finally to accept the 'counsel' of the citizens (which is in favour of releasing Antigone, too late, and also endorses the laws of the 'gods'), and the most basic 'political error' in the play is presented as the rejection of good advice from the democratic citizens' assembly (lines 1242-3). The *Bacchae*, in *Raisons*' condensed version, becomes an exploration of the inadequacy of behaviour based either on political force or on unthinking pleasure.

It is then their treatment of *Oedipus Tyrannos* that most intrigues me. From being a drama concerned with the discovery of incest and parricide, the play is almost turned into both an intellectual detective story and a development of the issues concenring law already broached.

By rapid juxtaposition of apparently unrelated lines, what emerges is a play predominantly concerned with a single question: the relation between the One and the Many (to use a formulation more familiar from pre-Socratic philosophy), the individual and collective identity and responsibility. An example can illustrate this. The whole prologue of *Oedipus* (lines 1-150) is compressed into some 15 lines (the italicisations are those of *Raisons*):

> Oedipus: *Children*, what do you *fear* or want? It would be hard not to *pity* suppliants like these.
>
> Priest: A pestilence is upon our city.
>
> Oedipus: I *pity* you, *children*. Your *several* sorrows each have *single* scope, but my spirit groans for *the city and myself and all of you* at once.
>
> Creon: I have good news though hard to bear.
>
> Oedipus: What you say leaves me uncertain whether to *trust* or *fear*. Speak your news to *all*.
>
> Creon: Apollo says it is the guilt of murder that pollutes the *city*. The murder of King Laius.
>
> Oedipus: Can no one tell us what happened?
>
> Creon: *All* Laius's servants were killed *save one*. He said the robbers they encountered were *many*; it was no man's *single* power.

> Oedipus: Come, *children*, call the *assembly*, and let it meet on the understanding that *I'll do everything.*

Even in this elliptical form, a number of themes are obviously at work: the relation between kinship, autocracy and *demo-cracy*; the role of pity and fear and trust; the various possible equations between one and many.

The play, in this version, is made to hinge on the moments when these themes are most plainly operative, but the most important turning-points are at line 845, where Oedipus fends off the truth concerning his murder of Laius by insisting that '*One* man cannot be the same as *many*', and the exchange between Oedipus and the messenger from Corinth, at lines 1014-20, which is retained almost in full:

> Messenger: Do you know that all your *fears* are empty?
>
> Oedipus: How is that, if they are father and mother and I their son?
>
> Messenger: Polybus was *no kin* to you.
>
> Oedipus: Was not Polybus my father?
>
> Messenger: *No more than I but just so much.*
>
> Oedipus: How can my father be my father as much as *one that's nothing to me*?
>
> Messenger: Neither he nor I begat you.

Once we connect this exchange to the theme of one being identical with many, it is clear that *Oedipus Tyrannos* is, for the authors of *Raisons*, essentially an inquiry into the nature of 'democratic' relations (i.e. those *not* based on kinship or territory) in which each citizen is equally related to every other.

While it may be the inappropriate 'fear' of Jocasta (1076) or the perhaps misapplied 'pity' of the shepherd (1178) which has brought about the opening situation, it is primarily Oedipus's angry refusal to recognise that he is *only one among many* that leads to his attempted repudiation of both truth and purification. In other words, the deepest 'error' presented in this play is the refusal to understand and accept the very nature of a 'democratic city'.

*

But what is the 'very nature of a democratic city'? How are we to think *that*? *Raisons* at this point gives us another Greek word and another quotation, in transliterated Greek, from Aristotle's *Nicomathean Ethics* Book I, 13, 1102a:

> *Eudaimonia*
>
> *estin he eudaimonia psykes energeia tis kat'areten teleian*

This is followed by a fairly standard translation:

> *happiness*: happiness is the activity of the soul in accordance with the highest virtue.

But then by various entries from a Greek dictionary:

eudaimon(os):— prosperous, fortunate; well-fated by the gods.

daimon: —a minor god.

daimoon: —skilled in something.

en-ergos: —busy, working; on active service (soldier);

—productive (land).

energazomonai: —to make, create; pursue a calling; labour; work for hire.

ergon: —a man's business, his work.

ergo: —to work, accomplish.

arete: —skill, excellence in workmanship (v. *tekne*).

teleios: —full, complete, fulfilled, perfectly done.

teleios aner: —full-grown, man with full rule and authority.

And finally by another quotation, in Greek, from Aristotle's *Politics*:

Man is a political animal.

Clearly, we are meant to attempt our own translation of the original phrase, our own working definitions of the terms 'happiness' and 'politics'. Something along these various lines might emerge:

> *Working well as a human being means being busy at doing or making something which demands a great deal of skill when you're good at it.*
>
> *Having a good time with your life means being able to do something well worth doing that demands and repays a lot of skilful effort.*
>
> *Happiness is an activity that demands and generates energy by putting the most complex skills and techniques we have to work on something.*
>
> *Being happy in one's work involves the most complete skill, the most demanding technique, and the better the technique the more productive and enjoyable the work will be.*

I've no idea if these are the kind of 'translations' *Raisons* is encouraging by its dictionary entries. Certainly they are far removed from any traditional reading of Aristotle!

On the one hand, that may not matter very much to the C.E.A.L. authors; on the other, it's possible to recognise an affinity between such translations and the implications of that laconic remark by Aristotle that 'in a tyranny only the tyrant can be happy.' If, for Aristotle, it is the *ergon*, the job, the point, the defining characteristic, the peculiar 'end', of a human being to 'make cities', to be 'political', then in a tyranny *only* the tyrant can fulfil that definition, has that *ergon*, so the rest of us cannot be 'happy': we are prevented from exercising our most complete skills and energies, those involved in 'making' the 'city'.

Given our contemporary understanding of—or respective reaction to—the terms 'happiness' and 'politics', this line of argument, or suggestion, seems sufficiently bizarre to make one suspect a joke. I wonder if the members of the Cercle Abnormale have ever spent a futile, depressing, frustrating, wearying evening attending a meeting of their local Labour Party Management Committee, or its French equivalent? One advantage of their procedure of declining to comment on the material they present is that they can avoid tackling such awkward thoughts.

Another is apparent from what immediately follows this section on *eudaimonia*.

A single page is headed 'A Short History of Happiness', and consists of just four quotations! The first is:

> . . true and perfect happiness is that which makes a man self-sufficient, powerful, worthy of reverence and renown, and joyful.
>
> Question: Do you imagine that there is any mortal and frail thing which can bring about a condition of this kind?
>
> Answer: No.

The only identifying information they give us is:

Boethius, b. 480, Consul 510, Master of the King's Offices, 520, imprisoned 525, wrote *The Consolation of Philosophy*, c. 530.

Pondering that skeletal career, perhaps no further comment is actually needed.

The second quotation is a composite passage from St Thomas Aquinas, *Summa Theologiae*, la 2ae, q.l, art. 6, q.3, art. 2, art. 5:

Question: Is everything a man wills on account of an ultimate end? Is it an activity? Of the theoretical or practical reason?

Response: The activity happiness is in the theoretical rather than the practical intelligence. Given that happiness is an activity, then it ought to be a man's best activity, that is to say when his highest power is engaged with its highest object. Man's mind is his highest power, and its highest object is divine good, an object for its seeing, not for its doing something in practice. Hence the activity of contemplating God is principal in happiness. And since, as Aristotle puts it, that strikes each man as himself which is best in him, such is the activity most proper and congenial to man.

The third is from Friedrich Schiller's *Letters on the Aesthetic Education of Man* (1793-5):

To declare it once and for all, Man plays only when he is in the full sense of the word a man, and *he is only wholly Man when he is playing*. We enjoy the pleasures of the senses simply as individuals, and the species which lives within us has no share in them; hence we cannot extend our sensuous pleasures into being universal, because we cannot make our own individuality universal. We enjoy

> the pleasures of knowledge simply as species, and by carefully removing every trace of individuality from our judgement; hence we cannot make our intellectual pleasures universal, because we cannot exclude the traces of individuality from the judgement of others as we do from our own. It is only the Beautiful that we enjoy at the same time as individual and species, that is, as *representatives* of the species. Sensuous good can make only *one* man happy, since it is based on appropriation, which always implies exclusion; it can also make this one man only partially happy, because the personality does not share in it. Absolute good can bring happiness only under conditions which are not to be universally assumed; for truth is only the reward of renunciation, and only a pure heart believes in the pure will. Beauty alone makes all the world happy, and every being forgets its limitations as long as it experiences her enchantment.

The final quotation is from Chapter V of John Stuart Mill's *Autobiography* (1873, posthumously):

> It was in the autumn of 1826. I was in a dull state of nerves, such as everybody is occasionally liable to; unsusceptible to enjoyment or pleasurable excitement; one of those moods when what is pleasure at other times, becomes insipid or indifferent; the state, I should think, in which converts to Methodism usually are, when smitten by their first 'conviction of sin'. In this frame of mind it occurred to me to put the question directly to myself: 'Suppose that all your objects in life were realised; that all the changes in institutions and opinions which you are looking forward to, could be completely effected at this very instant: would this be a great joy and happiness to you? ' And an irrepressible self-consciousness distinctly answered, 'No! ' At this my heart sank within me: the whole foundation on which my life was constructed fell down. All my happiness was

> to have been found in the continual pursuit of this end. The end had ceased to charm, and how could there ever again be any interest in the means? I seemed to have nothing left to live for.

The only biographical information on Mill given in *Raisons* is — quite bizarrely — that he was Member of Parliament for Westminster from 1865-8, and they refer us to, of all things, his 'Speech to the Electors of Westminster' and a letter to the *Daily News* 23 March 1865!

This is, one might surely think, a remarkably meagre cull even for a 'short' history of happiness! At the very least, I would want to add a passage from Karl Marx's *Economic and Philosophical Manuscripts* (1844) on 'the relationship of man to woman' as the index to 'the entire level of development of mankind', in demonstrating 'the extent to which the other, as human being, has become a need for man, the extent to which in his most individual existence he is at the same time a communal being.' Though perhaps I would then have to add some near-contemporary remarks from Kierkegaard's *Either/Or* (1843) on 'The Unhappiest Man' and 'The Aesthetic Validity of Marriage'—and possibly complement these two with an extract from their common intellectual ancestor, Hegel's essay 'On Love' in his early theological fragments.

As soon, in fact, as one thinks of further passages one recognises the advantage of *Raisons*' austere procedure: the trajectory they indicate, from 'politics' through philosophy and theology and aesthetics back to the atheist Mill's Benthamite dilemma, does probably encapsulate an essential movement — though one might recall that Mill at least found solace in Wordsworth, and this 'history' might well be read simply as a repertoire of permanent possible options.

The next quotation in Raisons' idiosyncratic organisation could only come from a history of *un*happiness — though no indication is given that we have actually switched 'histories'. It comes from Diodorus of Sicily (1st century AD):

> On the borders of Egypt and in the adjacent districts of Arabia and Ethiopia, there are many large gold mines worked intensively at great expense of misery and money. The rock is black with rifts and veins of marble so dazzling white that it outshines everything. This is where the gold is prepared by the overseers of the mines with a multitude of labourers. To these mines the Egyptian kings send condemned criminals, prisoners of war, also those who have fallen victim to false accusations or been imprisoned for incurring the royal displeasure, sometimes with all their kinfolk — both for the punishment of the guilty and for the profits which accrue from their labour. There they throng, all in chains, all kept at work continuously day and night. There is no relaxation, no means of escape; for, since they speak a variety of languages, their guards cannot be corrupted by friendly conversation or casual acts of kindness. Where the gold-bearing rock is very hard, it is first burned with fire, and, when it has been softened sufficiently to yield to their efforts, thousands upon thousands of these unfortunate wretches are set to work on it with iron stone-cutters under the direction of the craftsman who examines the stone and instructs them where to begin. The strongest of those assigned to this luckless labour hew the marble with iron picks. There is no skill in it, only force. The shafts are not cut in a straight line but follow the veins of the shining stone. Where the daylight is shut out by the twists and turns of the quarry, they wear lamps tied to their foreheads, and there, contorting their bodies to fit the contours of the rock, they throw the quarried fragments to the ground, toiling on and on without intermission under the pitiless overseer's lash. Young children descend the shafts into the bowels of the earth laboriously gathering the stones as they are thrown down, and carrying them into the open air at the shaft-head, where they are taken from them by men over thirty years, each receiving a

> prescribed amount, which they break on stone mortars with iron pestles into pieces as small as a vetch. Then they are handed on to women and older men, who lay them on rows of grindstones, and standing in groups of two and three they pound them to powder as fine as the best wheaten flour. No one could look on the squalor of these wretches, without even a rag to cover their loins, and not feel compassion for their plight. They may be sick, or maimed, or aged, or weakly women, but there is no indulgence, no respite. All alike are kept at their labour by the lash, until, overcome by hardships, they die in their torments. Their misery is so great that they dread what is to come even more than the present, the punishments are so severe, and death is welcomed as a thing more desirable than life.

This utterly sobering passage is, one hopes, familiar, if only from George Thomson's *The First Philosophers*, where he points out that this is

> the only example in classical literature of a writer who had the intellectual and moral courage to discover for himself and describe the mass of human misery on which his civilisation rested.

Thomson continues, incidentally:

> These, then, are the realities that first inspired the imagery that underlies so many Orphic parables of this life and the next — the Platonic Cave, in which men are chained from childhood hand and foot, and have never seen the daylight, and the topography of Tartarus, with its subterranean channels of water, mud, fire and brimstone; or the upper regions, under a clear sky, where the souls of the righteous are at rest . .

— enjoying the consolations of contemplative philosophy, no doubt.

As the next abrupt quotation might indirectly remind us, however, philosophy too could have its drawbacks. The passage is again taken from Aristotle's *Constitution* (XXXIV):

> The people shortly overthrew the Five Thousand. In the seventh year after the overthrow of the Four Hundred, the battle at Arginusae was fought. Thereafter, first the ten strategoi who won the battle were all condemned by a single vote, although some had not been present at the battle and others had been rescued by other ships; the people had been misled by those who were enraged by what had happened.

The incident happened in 406 BC, during the Peloponnesian war. Though the crucial sea-battle was won, a storm destroyed the returning fleet and the generals were held responsible for the ensuing deaths. Aristotle's account is both inaccurate and incomplete, but it does point to the problem which haunts Greek democracy—that the Assembly could indeed make 'tragic mistakes' when it was swayed by emotion, perhaps both rage and pity combined in this case. On this occasion the Assembly was also inquorate and broke its own standing orders.

Two other aspects of the incident are worth noting: that the slaves who took part in the battle were enfranchised, and that the President of the Assembly on the day of the condemnation of the generals was apparently the philosopher Socrates, who refused, unavailingly, to ratify the improper verdict. Seven years later Socrates himself was also condemned to death, for his endless questioning. The year 406 was also, incidentally, the year in which both Sophocles and Euripides died, bringing the great period of Greek tragedy to a close almost at the same moment as—on Aristotle's account—Athenian democracy entered its period of degeneration.

What connection we are meant to make between Diodorus's description of slavery and Aristotle's brief mention of the aftermath of the battle of Arginusae is perhaps made clearer by what immediately follows: the compressed versions of three of Euripides' plays mentioned earlier, *Women of Troy*, *Helen* and *Ion*. As with the previous 'versions' of Aeschylus and Sophocles, the tactic is, in effect, to re-write the plays in order to point up their connections with each other and with, it would seem, the problem of democracy. In *Raisons*' versions of the Euripides plays the emphasis is upon women, slaves, and children—precisely those categories excluded from Athenian *demo-cracy*.

Women of Troy is reduced to a series of confrontations between attempts to impose 'predefinitions' and attempts to refuse or avoid those predefinitions. Thus, Helen's refusal to accept her assigned role as guilty, as unfaithful, as responsible for the Trojan war, is contrasted with Hecuba's final acquiescence in her demotion from Queen to captive slave (after her foiled attempt at suicide, a last desperate assertion of her previous royal status). The play, of course, locates these women precisely *between* definitions: their old roles and status in Troy and the new lives that await them after the suspended moment of the play is over. But the centre, the pivot, of the play in this compressed version is the death of Astyanax, the infant son of Hector — killed not for anything the child has done but because he is defined in advance as avenger. The whole issue of fate and destiny is focused in this murder, an attempt to avert destiny; but as both the opening of the play (the old, old prophecies) and the ending (the gathering storm that will destroy the homeward fleet) remind us, destiny is still dominant in the story as a whole.

The *Helen*, on the other hand, hilariously undermines the entire 'story' of the Trojan war: Menelaus, shipwrecked in Egypt, finds that Helen never went to Troy at all and has been living in Egypt during the whole ten-year conflict, while a mere mirage of her had been foisted by the gods upon the deluded armies at Troy. The version offered in *Raisons* brings out the sheer arbitrariness of the relation between events, descriptions and 'definitions', from the opening words, establishing that 'this' (the arena of the theatre itself) is 'Egypt', to the closing reminder to the Athenians (during the war between Athens and Sparta) that the very name of 'Greeks' (*Hellenes*) derives from a Spartan: national identities are, in the end, only a matter of how we name ourselves and others. This lesson is instantiated in the play by the inefficacy of Menelaus's use of his own 'great name' in a country outside his sphere of power, and by the dispute between himself and his slave as to the meaning of both 'slave' and 'king'.

Finally, the uncertain status of names and identity is pointed up as central to the *Ion*, where the boy who is eventually to be called Ion has to decide between apparently irreconcilable accounts of his paternity and the future possible lives that would be determined by his 'choice' of father. (English readers may be more familiar with Eliot's reworking of the *Ion* in his *The Confidential Clerk*.)

With this version of the *Ion* we seem to have come full circle, back to the very first quotation from Aristotle in *Raisons des textes*, concerning the requirement that citizens be born of parents both of whom were citizens themselves. It is time to step back.

*

Pondering the sequence of extended quotations and compressed plays presented thus far in *Raisons des textes* — Marx, Wittgenstein, Aristotle's *Rhetoric*, *Poetics*, and *Athenian Constitution*, *The Suppliants*, *Antigone*, *Oedipus Tyrannos*, *isonomia* and happiness (*eudaimonia*), slavery, Arginusae, *Women of Troy*, *Helen*, *Ion*—we can, cautiously, move in various directions.

One central point is presumably obvious: that what we call 'democracy' in fifth-century Athens was organised in an extraordinarily elaborate and rational way, but it was also very strictly curtailed (excluding women and slaves) and was ultimately based upon two decidedly non-rational premises: the initial accident of birth and the final sanction of death. Full participation in the 'democracy' depended on the accident of being born the male child of Athenian citizens, while the entire structure of democratic government rested upon a horrendous edifice of slave-labour, specifically in the silver-mines which underpinned the Athenian economy and imperial power. One could also pick out, from the *mélange* of texts quoted, the importance of the jury system and allocation by lot, as a crucial *a*-rational and deliberately 'accidental' mechanism of democracy. Or one might emphasise the implied relation between the processes of democracy and the various functions of drama within Athenian society.

But there is a frustrating sense in which any such 'conclusions' are neither indicated by, nor even drawn from, the texts presented in *Raisons*. In order to arrive at those conclusions and certainly in order to think through their implications for Athenian democracy, the reader of *Raisons* already has to know, to some extent at least, the significance, the point, of those texts. But that surely requires a degree of specialist knowledge and expertise, and in that respect certainly not all readers of the book are 'equal'.

One is, in fact, acutely conscious of a paradox within the form of *Raisons des textes*: that while the argument one can elicit is concerned with radical democracy, the evidence (if that is what it is) they appeal to derives from that branch of learning which has peculiarly characterised the ruling elite of modem European societies: a 'classical education'. But if the reader has been excluded from or denied such an education, how is one meant to assess the worth of the evidence offered? Indeed, how is one to assess the 'argument', since mere juxtapositions provide the only 'links' ? It simply isn't clear whether we are being presented with an argument about history (the composite form of the first paragraph suggests otherwise) or perhaps merely with textual gestures, passages extracted from any historical context, for us to think about.

Yet why should we regard such passages as worth thinking about—and *how* should we 'think' about them? Are we simply to endorse those that in some way 'appeal to' us, or are we to judge them, somehow, 'rationally'? After all, it is the claim that all human beings are rational that has sometimes been offered as the basis of and justification for 'democracy'.

*

With these questions in mind we can now turn to Part II of this peculiar and challenging volume. Here we are first confronted with a section entitled 'A Short History of Reason', which consists of not even four passages but just four words or phrases!

> *akribeia*
>
> *Sic et Non*
>
> *cogito*
>
> *Age of Reason*

Perhaps indeed that is all that needs to be said on the topic! But how are we to take this sequence (or typology)? Is Aristotle's justified insistence, that in any inquiry one should (and can) only aim for that degree of precision (*akribeia*) appropriate to the object of inquiry, meant to be taken as contradicted by or ratified by the epochal work of Abelard (*Sic et non* - thus and not thus, yes and no, so and not so), opposing proofs from reason and dis-proofs from revelation, and *vice versa*, concerning the same item of doctrine? Or are we to see Abelard's maintained tension (Yes *and* No) as inevitably collapsing into the radical doubt and axiomatic rationalism of Descartes, the self-questioning and question-begging of 'I think'? Is the 'Age of Reason' (the English in the original alerts us to Tom Paine's tract rather than to Sartre's novel), that moment of revolutionary optimism in which Reason herself was enthroned as a goddess, to be seen as the final abandonment of the Aristotelian precept (one thinks of Edmund Burke's strictures) or as the triumphal (therefore disastrous?)

political application of the Cartesian scepticism and search for a new starting-point? Or should one finally read this curt 'short history' as suggesting a recovery of Aristotelian emphasis upon the objective and necessarily social character of all inquiry, after the long reign of personal self-questioning?

One could undoubtedly envisage different trajectories through these four 'moments', and one is inevitably prompted to query the selection and at least to question its historical limits. Are all pre-Socratic modes of thought also pre-rational? Is Immanuel Kant to be assimilated to the 'age of reason'? Has the post-Revolutionary era seen the implementation of 'reason' in human affairs— (surely not!) or rather its demise? After 1789 is the history of reason a blank? Yet C.E.A.L.'s own text is entitled *Raisons des textes*. Is there then a mode of 'literary' reason?

The bulk of Part II, headed *Raisons détectifs* (are other modes perhaps *raisons défectifs*?), is certainly concerned with literary texts, though the implied criteria of 'literary' are perhaps peculiar. Here the authors almost reverse their procedure in Part I: instead of highly selective quotations eclectically mingled from a variety of sources, they offer us just one long quotation from each of four works, followed by a commentary which requires us to bear in mind the rest of the relevant text. The texts themselves, however, are an odd mixture: Conan Doyle's first Sherlock Holmes short story, *A Scandal in Bohemia* (1891), Freud's first classic case history, *Dora* (written 1901, published 1905), Arthur Koestler's novel, *Darkness at Noon* (1938-40) and Bertolt Brecht's play *The Caucasian Chalk Circle* (c.1944).

The Conan Doyle quotation is actually the very first paragraph of the story:

> To Sherlock Holmes she is always the woman. I have seldom heard him mention her under any other name. In his eyes she eclipses and predominates the whole of her sex. It was not that he felt any emotion akin to love for Irene Adler. All emotions, and that one particularly,

> were abhorrent to his cold, precise but admirably balanced mind. He was, I take it, the most perfect reasoning and observing machine that the world has seen, but as a lover he would have placed himself in a false position. He never spoke of the softer passions, save with a gibe and a sneer. They were admirable things for the observer — excellent for drawing the veil from men's motives and actions. But for the trained reasoner to admit such intrusions into his own delicate and finely adjusted temperament was to introduce a distracting factor which might throw doubt upon all his mental results. Grit in a sensitive instrument, or a crack in one of his high-power lenses, would not be more disturbing than a strong emotion in a nature such as his. And yet there was but one woman to him, and that woman was the late Irene Adler, of dubious and questionable memory.

The commentary has a compact style:

> Wedlock suits Watson, but not the bohemian soul of Holmes which responds rather to the pretty problem of the King of Bohemia: a dis-honourable liaison to be disowned before legitimate marriage by the dispossession of a photograph, through theft, deception, force, and gold.

This is harsh, but arguably accurate. Holmes-lovers may, however, repudiate the implications of this curt description: ‘the hired secret agent of an unscrupulous foreign state’. Indeed, as Holmes' role is here described, it becomes indistinguishable from that of a more recent brand of agent:

> If it is important that justice should not only not be done, but also not even be seen not to be done, authority funds an agency to work outside the law, swearing to absolute secrecy and operating in disguise. The rationale for such a hidden hierarchy of law-breaking law-enforcement agencies is the need to prevent crime. A comprehensive data-bank on all potential criminals — i.e. an entry on every-one — will

> help prevent any truths emerging that might cast doubt on the conduct of those who authorise, condone, and finance theft and violence in their own interest.

One has to search the text rather un-sympathetically hard to justify that exegesis!

At this point, the CEAL authors promptly step outside the text to inform us that records of all reported crimes were initiated in England in the 1870s and that by the late 1970s an estimated 36,325,000 current names were available on the Hendon Police National Computer Unit, including 6.7 million 'criminal names' and some 3 million Special Branch files. They cite similar figures for most countries in Europe, then switch back to the Holmes story to focus upon Watson's 'moment of compunction and shame' before he chooses to 'release the rocket' rather than commit 'the blackest treachery' to Holmes, and the King.

Watson, on their reading, becomes potentially the moral centre of the tale, precisely because he allows, however momentarily, the 'softer passions' to 'remove the veil from Holmes' own motives and actions'; in doing so, he operates as 'latent grit in the finely adjusted machine, a crack in the most high-powered surveillance system the world has seen'. One purpose of that surveillance machine is, literally, 'repression' — of 'the woman, of sexuality, of Irene'.

After so much Greek in Part I, we are presumably expected to recognise the etymology of that name: *eirene*, 'peace'. And it is a kind of peace that Irene makes — by getting married herself, to a lawyer. In doing so, moreover, she even brings Holmes out of the shadows and endows him briefly with a quite different status as 'observer': as 'witness' to her wedding. But while witnessing a marriage ceremony is indeed a form of seeing, it is not one which can be assimilated to deduction (they cite Holmes's arrogant 'I see it, I deduce it'). At the end of the tale Holmes is left merely with an *image* of Irene, from which he is unable to deduce anything at all.

One is tempted after reading this commentary —of which there is much more, concerned mainly with the 'spuriousness and irrelevance' of Holmes' 'powers of reason', and with the various reversals of expectations, roles and levels in the tale—to complain, with Watson: 'at each successive instance of your reasoning I am baffled', though with the CEAL authors one cannot even add 'until you explain your process', for we seem to be drawn by this book into a process without any attempt at 'explanation'.

However, some links between *A Scandal in Bohemia* and Freud's *Dora* might be guessed at in advance: Freud, like Holmes, prides himself on successfully interpreting slight clues of behaviour and speech that others overlook; both operate on a mistaken assumption as to the actual love-object of the woman; both seem to succumb to an only half-admitted attraction; and it is the woman in each case who finds a way to 'close' it 'prematurely'. Yet *Raisons des textes* does not draw attention to these parallels. The passage chosen for quotation and commentary is Dora's 'second dream', though they modify Freud's own text to include, within square brackets, the 'addenda' and alternatives in Dora's later renditions of the dream, which Freud himself relegates to footnotes:

> I was walking about in a town which I did not know. I saw streets and squares which were strange to me. [I saw a monument in one of the squares.] Then I came into a house where I lived, went to my room, and found a letter from Mother lying there. She wrote saying that as I had left home without my parents' knowledge she had not wished to write to me that Father was ill. 'Now he is dead and if you like [There was a question-mark after this word, thus: 'like?'] you can come.' I then went to the station and asked about a hundred times: 'Where is the station?' I always got the answer: 'Five minutes.' I then saw a thick wood before me which I went into and there I asked a man whom I met. He said to me: 'Two and a half hours more' [alternative: 'Two hours']. He offered to accompany

> me. But I refused and went alone. I saw the station in front of me and could not reach it. At the same time I had the usual feeling of anxiety that one has in dreams when one cannot move forward. Then I was at home. I must have been travelling in the meantime, but I know nothing about that. I walked into the porter's lodge, and enquired for our flat. The maidservant opened the door to me and replied that Mother and the others were already at the Cemetery. [I saw myself particularly distinctly going up the stairs.] [After she had answered I went to my room, but not the least sadly, and began reading a big book that lay on my writing-table.]

Their 'commentary' begins with a summary of Freud's own interpretation of this dream, arranged in a quite entertaining fashion: as a musical composition, perhaps an opera score. Phrases from the dream form the libretto or vocal line, while the complex over-determinations Freud instances are arranged on successive staves, like the instrumental parts for an orchestra, so distributed as to indicate the chordal character of their interaction. It's an effective mode of illustration, but they perhaps stretch their point by then referring to Freud's mode of thinking and analysis as 'polyphonic'.

Something of what they intend by this term is made clearer by some parallels they then draw with the 'musical' structure and 'thematic' arrangement of various Modernist literary works: *Ulysses*, Pound's *Cantos*, Proust's *A la recherche* and Eliot's *Four Quartets*. Their suggestion seems to be that to 'read' these works or to respond to a dream-interpretation is closely akin to reading a score or listening to music: an alert but also shifting attention to simultaneous 'levels' of interacting notes, images, themes, sounds. The 'unconscious' would, on this model, be more like those sequences within a musical composition which escape our conscious attention yet which form a necessary part of its structure, its very intelligibility.

The applicability of this suggestion to our reading of Dora's dream is not immediately apparent, however, since we are next given two sets of dates, thus:

Dora's analysis:	Oct.-Dec. 1899
Interpretation of Dreams:	1900
	x
Interpretation of Dreams:	Nov. 1899
Dora's analysis:	Oct.-Dec. 1900

The second set, they claim, is historically accurate, but the first is that actually given in Freud's own account. Chapter 1 of the case-study opens 'In my *Interpretation of Dreams*, published in 1900' (the prefatory remarks also, incidentally, open with dates of Freud's works). Consistently in later life and in later textual additions to the case-study Freud 'misremembered' the date of Dora's analysis as 1899 instead of 1900. Not a parapraxis Freud ever analysed himself.

Indirectly at least, the CEAL authors imply an explanation for Freud's uncharacteristic memory-lapse, or persistent slip of the pen. They invite us to suppose that Dora herself had read the *Interpretation of Dreams*, probably in the last stages of her analysis. Given what we know of the actual 'Dora', this is indeed plausible. They then quote again the final addendum to her dream, pointing out that Freud himself normally regarded such addenda as crucially significant:

> After she had answered I went to my room, but not the least sadly, and began reading a big book that lay on my writing-desk.

Freud referred this 'dream-book' to an encyclopaedia Dora had guiltily read in March 1899, the clue to this interpretation being her familiarity with medical terminology 'known to physicians but not to laymen' which she must have 'derived from books', though her sexual know-ledge must also have been supplemented by 'a second and oral source of information'. Freud constantly returns to the question of this 'source' and suggests various possibilities—but consistently (as in other matters) fails to recognise Dora's own mother as a possible, even likely, source.

We are then invited by *Raisons* to re-read the complete dream-text and to see it as a (perhaps artificially and deliberately constructed!) text with two levels of meaning: that given in Freud's own interpretation (which *Raisons* does not actually dispute) and a second, almost overt, significance: as a dream-narrative of Dora's own experience of psychoanalysis! She had entered the strange world revealed by psychoanalysis, partly at the behest of her father but also (once her father's original motivation was sidestepped, by Freud) on her own behalf; after, in effect, asking many times in her life about her own sexuality and always being promised that she would know when she was a little older, she finally meets a man (Freud) who offers to accompany her on her path of self-knowledge — but he too only promises an ever-receding and postponed conclusion. (Slyly, the commentary quotes Freud: that analysing this dream 'had so far occupied two hours'. Or 'two-and-a half', possibly?) She therefore takes a successful short-cut, going it alone though with the help of a 'big book' intended for experts but not for laymen, supplemented with what she had already learned from her 'oral source', Freud's own treatment.

There is a certain outrageous humour in the notion that Dora *made up* her dream to fulfil Freud's wish to analyse her, but also used her knowledge derived from his own book to inform him that she no longer needed him — she opened the third session on the dream by telling Freud, to his surprise and resentment, that she was concluding the analysis.

The suggestion definitely sheds an amusing light on Freud's account of the interpretation process in those final sessions. We read that Dora conveniently provided him with a childhood-related accident that made her 'drag her foot' (almost a translation of the name 'Oedipus'), that 'every difficulty was resolved at a single blow by her prompt reply: Nine months later' (a well-prepared and far from innocent patness?), that Dora offered 'immediate confirmation' of his guesses, 'disputed [his] facts no longer', 'nodded assent, a thing which I had not expected', and in general 'listened to me without any other usual contradictions'. . . Surely, we almost say, Dora was finding it difficult not to burst out laughing as she beautifully led him down the path his own book on the interpretation of dreams had enabled her to map out for him!

How serious the CEAL authors are it is difficult at times to say, but they do raise a crucial issue for psychoanalysis: not simply the problem of circular feedback from the analysand's own advance knowledge of psychoanalytic procedures and interpretations (Dora having a doubly privileged position of priority in that respect) but the more difficult question of the distinction between 'expert' and 'layperson'. Freud's *Dora* text is littered with appeals to his own experience and extensive knowledge of other cases and to general 'rules' — but, arguably, he misses the main point in Dora's own case (she perhaps even tries to help him, with her significant references to pictures of 'nymphs' and the Madonna). Freud becomes, for Dora, superfluous, and in principle Freud could not argue otherwise, on the evidence of his own quasi-self-analysis in the *Interpretation of Dreams*. Later, Freud will insist upon the necessity of the trained analyst on the grounds that a negotiation of the 'transference' is essential to analysis — but it is precisely his own blindness to his own transference in the case of Dora that the text reveals.

Raisons des textes offers no conclusion to this commentary — except in the odd, displaced form of an 'Addendum to the History of Reason': the single word *Gedankenfreheit*, followed by the name Adorno. The German word is Freud's term normally translated as 'free association', but is also open to the rendering 'free speech', in the political sense. The reference to Adorno presumably directs us to his elaborate meditation on this word in his *Minima Moralia*:

> *Gedankenfreheit*: Freedom of thought — The displacement of philosophy by science has led, as we know, to a separation of the two elements whose unity, according to Hegel, constitutes the life of philosophy: reflection and speculation. The land of truth is handed over in disillusion to reflection, and speculation is tolerated ungraciously within it merely for the purpose of formulating hypotheses, which must be conceived outside working hours and yield results as quickly as possible. To believe, however, that the speculative realm has been preserved unscathed in its extra-scientific form, left in peace by the bustle of universal statistics, would be to err grievously. First, severance from reflection costs speculation itself dear enough. It is either degraded to a docile echo of traditional philosophical schemes, or, in its aloofness from blinded facts, perverted to the non-committal chatter of a private *Weltanschauung*. Not satisfied with this, however, science assimilated speculation to its own operations. Among the public functions of psycho-analysis, this is not the least. Its medium is free association. The way into the patient's unconscious is laid open by persuading him to forgo the responsibility of reflection, and the formation of analytic theory follows the same track, whether it allows its findings to be traced by the progress and the falterings of these associations, or whether the analysts—and I mean precisely the most gifted of them, like Groddeck—trust to their own associations. We are presented on the couch with a relaxed performance of what was once enacted, with the utmost exertion of thought, by Schelling and Hegel on the lecturer's podium: the deciphering of the

> phenomenon. But this drop in tension affects the quality of the thought: the difference is hardly less than that between the philosophy of revelation and the random gossip of a mother-in-law. The same movement of mind which was once to elevate its 'material' to a concept, is itself reduced to mere material for conceptual ordering. The ideas one has are just good enough to allow experts to decide whether their originator is a compulsive character, an oral type, or a hysteric. Thanks to the diminished responsibility that lies in its severance from reflection, from rational control, speculation is itself handed over as an object to science, whose subjectivity is extinguished with it. Thought, in allowing itself to be reminded of its unconscious origins by the administrative structure of analysis, forgets to be thought. From true judgement it becomes neutral stuff. Instead of mastering itself by performing the task of conceptualization, it entrusts itself impotently to processing by the doctor, who in any case knows everything beforehand. Thus speculation is definitively crushed, becoming itself a fact to be included in one of the departments of classification as proof that nothing changes.

A certain pattern, or score of themes, is perhaps emerging: the relations between expert and layman, reason and the 'softer passions', moral responsibility and the possibility of self-knowledge. But also some tentative parallels faintly suggest themselves: the search for self-knowledge recalls the Socratic 'know thyself'; Dora's refusal of definition echoes Helen's role in *Women of Troy*; her presentation of 'another' Dora even evokes the *Helen* play itself. But I confess to a certain bemusement at this stage, an inability to hear whatever polyphony is being composed for me.

Yet the peculiar 'reasoning' of this text does seem, somehow, to work on one, perhaps at some other level than conscious hearing. For example, after reading those earlier analyses of the fate of children in *Women of Troy* and *Ion*, I curiously found myself thinking of that strangely disturbing moment, nearly twenty-five centuries later, at the end of Chekhov's *Three Sisters* (1900, the year of Dora's analysis), when the stage-direction specifies the last 'action' of the play:

> Andrey enters. He is pushing the pram with Bobik sitting in it.

That moment always makes the theatre go chill for me. Bobik would have been seventeen or so in 1917. Think of that speech of Toozenbach in Act I:

> The time's come: there's a terrific thunder-cloud advancing upon us, a mighty storm that is coming to freshen us up! Yes, it's coming all right, it's quite near already, and it's going to blow away all this idleness and indifference, and prejudice against work, this rot of boredom that our society is suffering from. I'm going to work, and in twenty-five or thirty years' time every man and woman will be working. Every one of us!
>
> Chebutykin: I'm not going to work.

I think forward to Russia, twenty-five, thirty years later. Bobik would have been about thirty-five in 1935. What would the child have become? That child. And I *don't know* what I feel about Toozenbach's speech.

*

The authors of *Raisons* cannot, of course, be held responsible for my personal unconscious chords and connections across their text, but even so the very title of the next novel they comment on, *Darkness at Noon*, seemed highly apt at this point. They single out one long passage:

We have learnt history more thoroughly than the others. We differ from all others in our logical consistency. We know that virtue does not matter to history, and that crimes remain unpunished; but that every error has its consequences and venges itself unto the seventh generation. Therefore we concentrated all our efforts on preventing error and destroying the very seeds of it. Never in history has so much power over the future of humanity been concentrated in so few hands as in our case. Each wrong idea we follow is a crime committed against future generations. Therefore we have to punish wrong ideas as others punish crimes: with death. We were held for madmen because we followed every thought down to its final consequence and acted accordingly. We were compared to the Inquisition because, like them, we constantly felt in ourselves the whole weight of responsibility for the superindividual life to come. We resembled the great Inquisitors in that we persecuted the seeds of evil not only in men's deeds, but in their thoughts. We admitted no private sphere, not even inside a man's skull. We lived under the compulsion of working things out to their final conclusions. Our minds were so tensely charged that the slightest collision caused a mortal short-circuit. Thus we were fated to mutual destruction.

But how can the present decide what will be judged truth in the future? We are doing the work of prophets without their gift. We replaced vision by logical deduction; but although we all started from the same point of departure, we came to divergent results. Proof disproved proof, and finally we had to recur to faith—to axiomatic faith in the rightness of one's own reasoning. That is the crucial point. We have thrown all ballast overboard; only one anchor holds us: faith in one's self. Geometry is the purest realisation of human reason, but Euclid's axioms cannot be proved. He who does not believe in them sees the whole building crash.

Once reason itself has crashed, all that is left, apparently, is faith and ultimately only faith in oneself. But at this point (the second hearing, on the fifth day) in the logic of Rubashov's argument, it is the *a*-logical, precisely in the form of that enigmatic 'self', that 'grammatical fiction' of the first-person singular, that begins to intrigue and attract him. But the 'self' becomes apparent only as an uneasiness, a curiously palpable silence of response to certain (self-) questionings, in those muted monologues that are really dialogues of a special kind. In that silence, particularly, are to be heard echoes of repressed moral dilemmas and guilts: the sacrifice of other 'I's for which Rubashov has been responsible and which, for many readers, are sufficient to condemn him. Such readers concur with his final self-condemning plea of 'Guilty', but on quite other grounds than his accusers.

That common reading does not, however, satisfy the authors of *Raisons*. It is worth quoting the opening of their commentary on the quoted passage:

> This formulation of the argument secretes a paradox which undermines the strategy of the text. Rubashov's temptation to put himself in his opponent's position, to recognise the potential reversal of roles with Ivan, provides Koestler's governing device. He puts the reader in Rubashov's position, seeing the scene through his eyes, thinking within his premisses: a quasi-first-person narration.
>
> The final plea convinces us as true to Rubashov's own movement only if we too have become sufficiently inward to Rubashov's own commitment to endorse the justice of that plea according to the logic of that commitment, even though we are also invited to reject its justice in rejecting the premisses of that logic.
>
> Yet this double-movement rests on that questionable formal device: in adopting a quasi first-person viewpoint, the novel necessarily endorses *in advance* the position of the grammatical fiction while precluding the possibility of that historically objective perspective which is both premise and demand of the logic it rejects.

> Yet it is only through that very inwardness that the ostensible problem of the novel can be posed: only from within that particular personal history with its specific memories and its uncertainties concerning the future that the question of History's judgement can be plausibly rendered as a credible dilemma. Since the logic of the argument within the novel cannot by the novel's own admission be resolved by any logical argument concerning the claims of the grammatical fiction, it is only by this formal option of empathetic narrative that the logic of political commitment is ostensibly discredited. Thus the form doubly begs the questions posed.
>
> Only from the perspective of I can a mathematics which adds I to I and makes 2 be considered as *a priori* invalid.

Presumably that last reference is to the various passages in the novel on the 'algebraic' treatment of history.

This complicated, even tortuous, commentary can be inadequately summarised as saying that despite the appearance of two positions engaged in a struggle for supremacy within the novel — ruthless determination versus moral judgement — one position has already been endorsed in advance by the very narrative mode of the novel.

But this is surely to reject the very possibility of a specifically novelistic treatment of these issues. A novel can only present an issue as experienced and debated by specific individuals in a specific situation, but then at least some aspects of the issue are 'already' settled or taken for granted by those individuals, not least the genuine impossibility for those individuals of an answer to any dilemmas in terms of the actual future judgement of history.

It's worth remarking that any search for moral premisses ignores this simple social fact. One might, of course, argue that a fictional treatment of this issue is inappropriate on other grounds: that what is at stake in the 'sacrifice' of an individual must always be an actual individual, one therefore situated in a myriad of ways more complicated than any form of fiction can adequately deal with.

But in fact *Raisons des textes* is not concerned with the problems, or appropriateness, of fiction; its interest is fixed on logic. The commentary continues, with its own compact mode of logic:

> Yet if the reader is brought to a recognition of the 'justice' of Rubashov's plea according to the logic of the political position Rubashov continues to maintain, and if one consequence of that position is indeed a legal system by which Rubashov can be condemned not for what he did but for the 'consequent logic' of what he believed (where the distinctions between opposition, assassination and civil war are, rightly, judicial subtleties), then a reader who judges that legal system and its consequences to be unjust is thereby placed in a position parallel to Rubashov's own.
>
> Either the reader accepts the consequent logic of his own judgement upon that system and is thereby committed to an opposition which (in any real world) may not stop short of war, or in recoiling from such practical opposition accepts that system, at least for others, thereby conceding to Rubashov a consistency the reader has evaded.
>
> Yet the legal system which condemns Rubashov cannot be judged unjust merely against the norm of some other legal system—since that too would have to be judged to be the norm; nor by any appeal to history, since that would be to re-embark on Rubashov's own trajectory; and to judge by any form of appeal to one's own infallibility would merely be to re-enter that same trajectory at a later stage.
>
> In judging Rubashov's plea we therefore have to judge Rubashov rather than the system which accepts and endorses his plea, yet we can only judge Rubashov by the criteria which we recognise as governing our own self-judgements, and they necessarily derive from our

> own first-person viewpoint, precluded as we are from attaining an objective perspective or historical judgement upon our own lives. Thus the reader is left by the logic of this novel with no consistent basis for judgement.

Tightly wrought as it is, I have two major objections to this argument. First, that neither the novel nor actual history convinces me that it was a 'consequent logic' of Rubashov's kind of commitment that political opposition should be eradicated by executions. Second, I am unpersuaded that an objective perspective upon one's own life is wholly precluded — though I recognise the problem of locating the grounds for that objectivity.

Oddly, the commentary itself argues that all legal systems eventually have recourse to a notion of 'objective guilt', in the crime of 'treason', since what makes an act specifically treasonable is not simply the character of the act or the intention of the agent but the fact of the accused being a citizen of this State rather than of some other. That 'objective' fact is thereby legally presumed to involve a 'consequent logic' of commitment to that political-legal system; conversely, it is suggested, any deliberate rejection of a specific law implicates one in a consequent logic of, if necessary, a rejection of the entire legal, and ultimately political, system of which one is 'objectively' a member.

Involved in any self-judgement, then, is a judgement concerning the State one chooses, or would choose, to commit oneself to. Again, one is rather uneasily aware of a distant echo back at this point to the discussions in Part I, of the Athenian constitution, of the relations between juries and law-making, of Socrates, and even perhaps of *Oedipus Tyrannos* — another victim of 'objective guilt' who learned, tragically, that the structure of the State is such that a judgement upon unknown others implicates oneself.

*

The issues that *Raisons des textes* successively forces upon us seem ferociously entangled with each other. One wishes, even desperately, for disentanglement and elucidation, for a clarity and lucidity of analysis that both the structure and the style of this book seem deliberately to refuse. Certainly the authors have not chosen to write a treatise in political philosophy or a constitutional handbook (though they began by quoting from a combination of both), yet the disparate and mainly literary texts they focus on do seem, for them, to operate in a register akin to those familiar modes of inquiry and analysis.

Perhaps by their very obliquity and opacity, they are prompting us to a difficult recognition of the nature of our own *actual* 'political' thinking: which rarely takes the form of professional philosophical analysis, expert constitutional inquiry, or even knowledgeable journalistic commentary (though we may need to call upon all these skills) but rather operates 'polyphonically': a disturbingly opaque interplay of passion, logic, rhetoric, commitment, moral judgement, emotion—and, overall, a peculiar form of 'reasoning' in which the conclusions are sometimes only a step towards acknowledging the premisses from which we know we should have begun and upon which we feel bound to act.

*

The final commentary in *Raisons* is upon the *Epilogue* to Brecht's play, *The Caucasian Chalk Circle*, the closing words of the Singer-Narrator:

> And after this evening Azdak disappeared and was never seen again.
> But the people of Grusinia did not forget him and often remembered
> His time of judgement as a brief Golden Age that was almost just.
> But you, who have listened to the story of the Chalk Circle

> Take note of the meaning of the ancient song:
> That what there is shall belong to those who are good for it, thus:
> The children to the maternal, that they thrive;
> The carriages to good drivers, that they are driven well;
> And the valley to the waterers, that it shall bear fruit.

The commentary initially concentrates on reminding us not only of how, as the epilogue indicates, two stories are intersected in the structure of the play — the tale of Grusha and the child, and the story of Azdak the judge — but also of how, in many of its local details and arrangements, the various episodes, sub-scenes and gestures echo each other across the texture of the play. That Azdak characteristically hears two cases simultaneously, his unpredictable judgements interweaving apparently disconnected issues, is offered as exemplary of the play's whole organisation. (Here again we can sense the CEAL authors endorsing a peculiarly 'polyphonic' mode.) Yet Azdak's rulings are not wholly unpredictable: they are clearly class-based judgements, invariably for the poor against the rich. Yet it is characteristic of the play (some would say a weakness) that these class-preferences are dramatically reinforced by an appeal to the audience's simpler emotional responses: the rich are presented as arrogant and unpleasant, while the poor in at least some cases (the old widow and the good-hearted bandit) are sentimentally portrayed.

The kind of judgement being invited or evoked is certainly class-based but supplemented by what could be variously termed (judged as) 'moral', 'emotional' or 'empathetic' judgement. The *Raisons* commentary opts for 'empathetic', arguing that empathy is the real basis of any actual solidarity or class-feeling between the poor and oppressed — an imaginative identification with others' suffering—rather than the rationalistic basis sometimes proposed, of a common recognition of interest or generalised self-interest based on one's own class-position.

Their point is that commitments, positions or arguments based on (self-)interest are necessarily modified as soon as one's 'interest' is even marginally differentiated from that of others: any 'solidarity' on that basis is fragile and temporary. Empathy, however, to some extent can both over-ride and out-last self-interest. They enroll Grusha in their argument, maintaining that it is precisely her empathy with the child that commits her to saving it in the first place:

> For a long time she sat with the child.
>
> Evening came, night came, dawn came.
>
> Too long she sat, too long she watched
>
> The soft-breathing, the little fists
>
> Till towards morning the temptation grew too strong.

It is empathy too which makes her let go of little Michael in the tug-of-war contest with the 'real' mother in the circle ('Am I to tear him to pieces? I can't do it! '). Empathy overrides rational consideration, both of self-interest and the apparent interest of the child (that she should 'prove' herself the 'real' mother by not letting go).

I remain somewhat unconvinced by this argument, both in its general claims and in its application to Grusha. Class-empathy seems to me as fragile and as temporary as any other kind of class-identification, and indeed — as I remarked earlier in relation to Aristotle's *Poetics* — as any other kind of 'empathy'. And in Grusha's case Brecht's own commentary (which *Raisons* does not cite) deploys quite other terms: maternal instincts, love and even interest. He also uses 'productive' in an odd sense:

> Her maternal instincts lay Grusha open to troubles and tribulations which prove very nearly fatal. All she wants of Azdak is permission to go on producing, in other words to pay more. She loves the child; her claim to it is

> based on the fact that she is willing and able to be productive.

And elsewhere, in a 'dialogue' on the play, we find this:

> B: . . the trial scene isn't about the maid's claim to the child but about the child's claim to the better mother. And the maid's suitability for being a mother, her usefulness and reliability are shown precisely by her level-headed reservations about taking the child on.
>
> R: Even her reservations strike me as beautiful. Friendliness is not unlimited, it is subject to measure. A person has just so much friendliness — no more, no less — and it is furthermore dependent on the situation at the time. It can be exhausted, can be replenished, and so on.
>
> W: I'd call that a realistic view.
>
> B: It's too mechanical for me: unfriendly. Why not look at it this way? Evil times make humane feelings a danger to humanity. Inside the maid Grusha the child's interests and her own are at loggerheads with one another. She must acknowledge both interests and do her best to promote them both. This way of looking at it, I think, must lead to a richer and more flexible portrayal of the Grusha part. It's true.

Only if the *Raisons* notion of 'empathy' can incorporate these more complex considerations could it serve to make the link required by the play between the story of the circle and that other 'second' story which frames the play: the debate between two collective farms in the post-war Soviet Union.

Yet even the relation between the chalk circle verdict and the decision over the disputed valley is less simple than it might appear. In that dispute there is no *class* difference upon which to base a preference—which crucially distinguishes it (as a political problem) from Azdak's judgements, yet no compelling parallel can really be drawn between the respective positions of Grusha and Abashvili and the fruit-growers and goat-breeders. It is, after all, the latter who, like Grusha, base their claim on 'love' and even upon having 'tended' the land. On the other hand, the fruit-growers can claim to have defended the valley against the German 'Ironsides' during the war. *Raisons* quotes an early draft of the epilogue in which the goat-breeders explicitly repudiate the suggested parallel:

> how dare you compare us . . with people like that Natalia Abashvili of yours, just because we think twice about giving up our valley.

Yet the final version of the epilogue does seem to make a direct parallel:

> The children to the maternal, that they thrive . .
>
> And the valley to the waterers, that it shall bear fruit.

Despite this, I have known audiences who were convinced after a performance that the decision had gone the *other* way — perhaps swayed by the rather more attractive characterisation of the Old Man who offers the barely-tolerable cheese.

Raisons rather side-steps this problem, and concentrates instead on an analysis of how the decision is actually reached in the *Prologue*. Returning to a favourite theme, they emphasise the minimal role played by the 'expert' from the capital, while highlighting the mingling of rhetoric, appeals to sentiment, use of humour, arguments about legal rights, etc., which all enter into the discussion and influence the outcome. But they then single out the quotation from Mayakovsky: — 'The home of the Soviet people shall also be the home of Reason' — as signalling the decisive argument, the real turning point: the fact that the detailed plans for the irrigation development are based upon the specific material features of the valley.

In a curious way this does seem to be true in Brecht's composition of the scene, yet it is difficult to see quite why this should be the decisive factor. I suspect it is because the very precision of specification (sometimes given little emphasis in production: 'Why is there a fall of 66 feet? ', 'This rock is to be dynamited! ' 'They force the water down here, that's clever! ', and so on) indicates that the project can only happen 'here' (whereas the goat-cheese can possibly be produced elsewhere?) and that in itself shows a close respect for the particular materiality of the land which is akin to, and part of, that 'love' for the land which is the main claim of the original villagers. Nevertheless, I can imagine a version of this discussion in which the decision did go the other way—and it would be remarkably easy to adapt the epilogue's final line accordingly. Brecht's own comment (again ignored by *Raisons*) is illuminating:

> *The Caucasian Chalk Circle* is not a parable. Possibly the prologue may create confusion on this point, since it looks superficially as if the whole story is being told in order to clear up the argument about who owns the valley. On closer inspection however the story is seen to be a true narrative which of itself proves nothing but merely displays a particular kind of wisdom, a potentially model attitude for the argument in question. Seen this way, the prologue becomes a background which situates the practicability and also the evolution of such wisdom in an historic setting.

Brecht's comment might even be adapted to apply to the basic organisation of *Raisons des textes* itself: it certainly 'proves' nothing, but does perhaps 'display' a certain mode of grappling with a problem (*sic et non*, yes *and* no?), a potentially model attitude for a kind of 'reasoning' that would itself be 'democratic'. (Whether it presents a 'narrative' is another matter!) Disappointingly, *Raisons*' own conclusion, not only to their Brecht commentary but to the whole book, is rather less complex than Brecht's.

They basically suggest that the necessary components of 'democratic reasoning' — i.e. the mode of political argument and decision-making appropriate to a fully classless society — would be a combination of 'empathy' and 'material knowledge', the first being a capacity for imaginative identification with and recognition of the needs of another, and the second a precise grasp of and respect for the material possibilities of the resources available (*akribeia*?). Yet this is surely only a disguised version of the traditional marxist position, a mere displacement or re-labelling of, respectively, 'class consciousness' and that practical knowledge and skill attributed to those who concretely produce the material necessities of social life.

In a way, the ending of the book is not only simple and unsatisfying but actually sentimental: the final page consists of a photograph of a quite delightfully happy and laughing child, flanked on one side by two quotations from Wittgenstein's *On Certainty*:

> Children do not learn that books exist, that armchairs exist, etc. etc. — they learn to fetch books, sit in armchairs, etc. etc.
>
> Is it wrong to say: 'A child that has mastered a language-game must *know* certain things'? If instead of that one said: 'must be able to *do* certain things', that would be a pleonasm, yet this is just what I want to counter the first sentence with.

And, on the other, by the quotations from Wittgenstein and Marx with which the book began:

> A child has much to learn before it can pretend. Does not the true character of each epoch come alive in its children?

Yet even this last gesture of repetition reminds us that this curious text greatly exceeds its unsatisfactory conclusion. Its own polyphonic structure pushes us away from simply seeking a 'conclusion' to a clearly linear argument. The various uncompleted strands, the only half-acknowledged echoes (Michael's fate in *Chalk Circle* is surely another reworking of that of Ion or even Astyanax), refuse to shape into an 'expert' or 'authoritative' statement. Each reader is left to construct from these materials an overall response—an oddly, and even infuriatingly, 'democratic' gesture! Yet at the same time the various devices of the text and the texts chosen for compression or commentary seem to imply that what we have generally classed as drama and literature may, in at least some cases, be read primarily as modes of (initiation into) 'political' thought.

For example, in trying to grasp the relation between the personal and the structural in those resistantly opaque and often tragic dramas of the Athenian *polis* we are learning, as once the young *ephebes* did, how to participate appropriately (yet precisely not as 'experts' in a later sense) in the processes of democratic decision and of law-making. *Raisons des textes* certainly shares something of that same opacity, and may even have the overall 'shape' of a tragedy, but — like the audiences at the Athenian festivals — I perhaps have had to learn from responding to the performance itself the grounds upon which I might judge it.

*

Each reader will respond differently. This reader found his mind revolving two main issues. The first is how actually to organise a genuinely class-less democracy. The usual proposals concentrate on such matters as mandated delegates, single-issue representatives, complex hierarchies of elected committees, or forms of localised 'direct' or 'mass' decision. If a role for 'experts' or 'professionals' is retained, it is seen often as that of providing alternative or opposing plans and detailed proposals, between which a choice can be made, with full information publicly accessible.

Yet one merely has to skim, say, Harold Wilson's frenetic memoirs of his premiership from 1964 to 1970 to realise not only the ludicrously crowded personal timetables enforced by our present arrangements but also the appalling amount of 'information' that has currently to be assimilated by the political professional.

Given the present intricate global interactions, economic, diplomatic, military, it does not seem feasible to envisage any effective forms of direct democracy, of non-hierarchical responsibility structures, or even of public access to and assimilation of 'full relevant information'. Nor is it clear that any future class-less social formations would constitute *less* complexly interrelated elements in a global order.

But even beyond these formidable problems of concretely realising democratic participation (rather than occasional electoral transmission of political power), there remains the acutely difficult but quite crucial issue of *the modes of argument and thought* appropriate to a fully democratic political system: how does one (or the many) *think politically*?

It is here perhaps that *Raisons des textes* suggests some possible emphases, though no more than that. A number of themes resonate together: childhood, self-knowledge, self-judgement, active learning, non-'rational' modes of thinking, the relations between 'expert' knowledge and 'lay' insight in certain areas, the ability (in Brecht's words) to think *within* the flow as well as *above* the flow. If democratic participation and responsibility is still seriously possible, a crucial pre-condition is adequate 'political education' *before* full adult-hood, a learning by both practice and 'pretending', and the most appropriate mode of such 'education' would seem—if we acknowledge the Athenian lesson—to be through 'dramatic' and 'aesthetic' experience.

This would involve, not only in schools but necessarily there, a sustained involvement in 'judging' 'political' plays and fictions, including constructing and performing political dramas, in *practising* responsibilities in both real and 'pretend' situations, in learning rhetorical and persuasive skills as well as those of rational calculation. The qualifying term 'political' in this context need not indicate a narrow focus upon the immediately topical and controversial, as the treatment in *Raisons* of Greek plays indicates! Indeed, those classical dramas may well be a crucial component of such an educative process, raising as they do problems of self-knowledge, of the relations between State and individual, conflicts between law and moral responsibility—in ways which demand genuinely difficult judgements.

If such an educational programme recalls in some of its elements precisely that 'classical education' (Greek, rhetoric, debating) associated with a discredited 'public school' system, that is perhaps not surprising. In certain limited ways—as one would indeed expect—the ruling elite has successfully used its educational system to train its children in the exercise of political power (over and above the social 'superiority' they were allegedly bred to), and the traditional concentration on 'the classics' was by no means mistaken. It is perhaps the very contradiction between the implicitly 'democratic' character of the material studied and the restrictions upon democratic participation sustained by that ruling elite which increasingly condemned 'classical education' to decadence and irrelevance. Perhaps a recovery of the political significance and function of those 'aesthetic' modes which first emerged within Athenian democracy is now possible. But of course the point of such an educational focus would be frustrated if the real exercise of political responsibility were denied in adult life.

Here again, there may possibly be lessons available from the Athenian reliance upon allocation to legal, political and administrative positions by lot, a principle we retain only in the case of juries. Radically to extend that principle, alongside electoral procedures and 'professional expertise', might indeed be possible at both local and national levels, in the form of a proportional composition of local councils or the 'allotment' of some members of reconstituted 'second chambers' and 'select committees'.

The necessary continuation of 'political education' into adult life might well involve tackling the problem of 'assimilating' 'information' along related lines. Even at present some of the most impressive and memorable work on television, for example, has been in the form of dramatic treatments of political principles, issues and problems. (The work of Trevor Griffiths, from *Occupations* to *Bill Brand*, has been in some respects exemplary.) Informed participation at a public inquiry into, say, a proposed nuclear power station can involve the assimilation of (to cite one recent case) 22,000 pages of documentation. Yet one can envisage competing dramatisations of the issues involved, each controlled by—and partly subject to judgement in terms of—the aesthetic demand to present the strongest possible arguments and counter-arguments within the work.

Here we can recall Aristotle's remark that 'Persuasion is achieved by the speaker's personal character when the speech is so spoken as to make us think him credible.' That is a controlling consideration not only for the creation of 'characters' but for the overall credibility of a work: the composition of a serious work of art involves a commitment to the fullest possible engagement with, and not evasion of, the issues tackled.

That difficult demand upon the 'character' of the artist is different from the demands placed upon either the professional politician or the expert, if only because, in Brecht's words, a 'true narrative' of itself 'proves nothing but merely displays a particular kind of wisdom, a potentially model attitude for the argument in question.' It is partly from those Greek dramas of two millennia ago that we have inherited that crucial criterion of serious art: 'in a certain respect', as Marx remarked, they do indeed 'count as a norm and as an unattainable model' — un-attainable, that is, until we recover and go beyond the democratic impulse and forms of social organisation which fostered them and which they helped sustain.

Raisons des textes obviously cannot be judged a successful work, but in trying to respond thoughtfully to its own 'polyphonic' mode of thinking I at least have been brought to confront —with perhaps equal lack of success — a range of formidably difficult problems, including the peculiar and frustrating problem of *how* I am to think about them and what would, in practice, actually qualify me to do so. For that prompting, I respect—however critically—the impulse behind this curious book.

Printed in Great Britain
by Amazon